MY BEST TO YOU

AT EVENTIDE

Volume 2 of a Devotional Series

Rev. Donald C. Hancock

This edition is published by Donald C. Hancock
of Augusta, Georgia.
Printed in United States of America

If you enjoy this book, you might also enjoy my other books, which can be found and purchased on Amazon Books:

"A Message For All Time" …A romance novel of World War II.
"My Best To You Each Morning"....My previous devotional book.
"From My Heart To Yours"...My favorite short stories.
"A Variety of Gems"Poems, short stories, and essays. A collection.
"A Variety of Gems, Vol. 2"....A second volume of the above.

DEDICATION

I lovingly dedicate this second book of devotional thoughts to my wife, Finetta, who has always been the wind beneath my wings, and to Bob Scaggs, the Director of my Sunday School Department, who gave me the privilege of bringing these devotionals to our Sunday School Department. I would also like to acknowledge the men and women of that Department, who listened to these devotionals initially and encouraged me to continue.

I am also grateful to the senior groups in the local churches that have allowed me to come and speak to them, using some of the devotionals found in these books. They encouraged me to continue and also to add this new book.

Lastly, I dedicate this and all of my writings to God, Who has given me all that I have.

My Best To You At Eventide
Vol. 2 of a Devotional Series

Table of Contents

INTRODUCTION

Several years ago I retired as a Chaplain in a State School for the Developmentally Disabled, where I had ministered full time for 21 years. Before that I had been a Pastor for 14 years. So, after retirement I was delighted to be asked, about twice a month, to prepare a ten minute devotional for my own Sunday School Department at First Baptist Church of Augusta, Georgia. The department is made up of Senior Adults, men and women, who accepted my offerings graciously.

Since each devotional was prepared prayerfully and with a great deal of thought and preparation, I thought that it might be helpful to other folks. So, when I had collected 40 of those devotionals, I published them in a little book called, "My Best To You Each Morning", hoping it would be helpful for your own devotional use. I also prepared a 30 minute program and offered to present some of my devotionals to other senior groups in local churches. Both the book and the program have been so well received that I have prepared this second volume of devotionals. I hope that it will also prove to be helpful. That is my purpose in offering it to you. Rev. Donald C. Hancock, Augusta, Georgia. November, 2012.

CHAPTER 1: EASTER MORNING, AND YOU ARE THERE!

Most of you remember a very successful television series of the 1950's, called "You Are There".They would take such historic events as the assassination of President Lincoln or the burning of the Airship Hindenburg and set up the program as if Walter Cronkite, or some other announcer, was actually covering the happening first hand!

I would like for you to use your imagination and be a part of such a presentation of the "Day that Christ arose from the dead - the first Easter day!

"Hello ladies and gentlemen. This is Abraham Levine reporting for C.B.S., and we are in Jerusalem in the year 33 AD. And You Are There! It is in the early evening of the first day of the week. Ordinarily people would have been going back to their homes by now but everything is still in a state of excitement after the events of this morning. Everyone is talking about the same thing! It has been reported that a Jew by the name of Jesus, called the 'Nazarene' by some, was executed by the Romans but apparently arose from the dead! That's right! They are saying that when they went back to the grave site this morning, his body simply was NOT there!

"Here is a Roman soldier. I will see if I can find out anything from him...Hello, Sir, can you tell me anything about this story that a man allegedly arose from the dead this morning?"

"Well, yes, I can tell you what I know at least. It was my men who actually crucified this man in the usual method of Roman execution. I DO know that he was dead, because I examined his body. But his death was very mysterious. Right after he expired, there was an awful earthquake and it was totally dark until about 3:00 o'clock. I found myself saying, 'This really must have been the son of God!'

"Then, some of the Jews asked Pilate if he would post a guard at the tomb, because they were afraid that someone would steal the body in order to make a martyr of him. But Pilate just gave them permission to post their own guard, which they did. But, somehow the body was missing! The followers of Jesus do claim that he was raised from the dead!"

"Really! Where can I find some of his followers now?"

"Actually, there are some of the main ones in that little group over there!"

"Oh, excuse me, Sir. Are you one of the followers of the man known as Jesus?"

"Yes! yes! yes! I am so happy to say, 'yes' now! You see, forgive me for being so excited, but I did an awful thing before. When Jesus was being tried by the High Priest, a young girl asked me that very same question and I was so afraid then that I said, 'NO!'. I really let Jesus down. I was so ashamed!."

"But why are you so different now? - By the way, you are....?"

"Sir, I am Peter. The reason that I am so different is, first of all, Jesus is alive! Really alive! I have seen Him. I have touched Him. Also, He knew about my betrayal and yet He forgave me! He still loves me! "

"Sir, you actually touched him? You are really sure that it was him?

"Yes Sir. I saw nail holes in his hands. I saw the actual place where a spear went into his side!"

"May I ask who else is in this group?"

"They call me Mary Magdalene. I was one of the women who found the tomb empty. We were so confused. Who would stoop so low as to rob the grave of our Master? Then, two angels told us that Jesus had been raised from the dead. We went back and told the Apostles. They really didn't believe us at first. But Jesus actually appeared to all of us later!"

"So, you are saying that all of the Apostles saw him and that they were all sure that it was really Jesus?"

"Well, all but Thomas. He wasn't there the first time Jesus appeared. So he didn't believe us."

"So, Thomas didn't believe?"

"Well, now he does. Here he is. You can talk with him yourself."

"You are Thomas?"

"Yes Sir. I am actually embarrassed to remember how I acted. But it just didn't seem reasonable to me that what they were saying could be true - that Jesus was actually alive again. I just could not believe such a thing! But, as soon as I saw him - immediately - I knew beyond the shadow of a doubt that it was He!"

"And I knew too!"

"And you are....?"

"I am His mother. I knew as soon as I saw Him smile, that He was my son and that He was all right again. As soon as I saw Him alive, everything seemed to fit together. The angel had told me that my son would be the Son of God. Another angel had told my husband, Joseph, the same thing."

"So, all of you really believe that the one you saw was Jesus and that he really was alive again?"

"Yes, yes, yes - all of us! And not only that He is alive but that He is our Savior and Master of our lives! And He promised that the Spirit of God would lead us into the future, and we can hardly wait to see what is going to happen!"

"Well, there you have it! A report on what happened today when Jesus, called the 'Nazarene', was not only crucified but, apparently, was raised from the dead. This is Abraham Levine, reporting for C.B.S.

And YOU WERE THERE!

CHAPTER 2: FIRST AND SECOND HAND EXPERIENCE

There are three songs that I would like to share – three songs that seem to have nothing in common. But they do have a common thread. The first song you know and you can sing it from memory - "The White Cliffs of Dover".

"There'll be blue birds over the white cliffs of Dover tomorrow, just you wait and see.

There'll be love and laughter and peace ever after tomorrow when the world is free.

The shepherd will tend his sheep, the valley will bloom again,

And Jimmy will go to sleep in his own little room again.

There'll be blue birds over the white cliffs of Dover tomorrow just you wait and see.

The second song is "Take me out to the ball game!" Strange that I would mention that one next to the first one. But, humor me for a few minutes and I will tell you how they are alike.

"Take me out to the ball game, take me out with the crowd.

Buy me some peanuts and cracker jack, I don't care if we never get back,

Let me root, root, root for the home team,

If they don't win it's a shame.

For it's one, two, three and you're out

At the ole ball game!"

These first two songs have one thing in common. The composers did them the hard way – from second hand information. "The White Cliffs of Dover" was written by an American, Nat Burton. Written in 1941, it was inspired by the battle for Britain, because the cliffs of Dover was the area where the British pilots of the R.A.F confronted the invading German airplanes in that relentless battle. The song gave a great deal of courage and hope to all of the allied nations during World War II. But, as beautiful and helpful as it was, the American writer had never, ever seen the cliffs of Dover. He had not been within 3000 miles of that area. He had composed the song totally on the basis of second hand information.

The second song, "Take me out to the ball game", was written by a song writer, Jack Norworth, in 1908. He was riding on the subway in New York City when he saw a sign that said, "Game Today!", speaking of the New York Yankees. It inspired him and he jotted down the words to the song. It immediately became a big hit and has been sung during the seventh inning "stretch" at literally millions of baseball games since that time. But Jack did it the hard way. You see, at the time he wrote the song, he had never experienced what it was really like to sit and watch a game. He had composed the song totally on the basis of second hand information.

But the third song was very different. The composer was also a song writer. Stuart Hamblen was the son of a Methodist minister, but, once he left home, his life took a downward turn. He intended to go to college to become a teacher. But he quickly found out that he was much more attracted to "western"music and radio. He began to sing with a group on the radio and then got into the movies, doing cowboy songs. He got to know Gene Autry, Roy Rogers, and John Wayne. He also started drinking alcohol and gambling, and these two habits became an addiction.

Then, in 1949, a young evangelist came to Los Angeles and held an evangelistic rally. Stuart's wife persuaded him to go with her and Stuart was converted. It was there that he found God and also found the strength to end his addictions. His life was totally changed after that experience. Billy Graham later said that Stuart's conversion was a turning point in the success of the Los Angeles meeting, because so many people were aware of the change in this very popular celebrity's life.

About three years later, Stuart and John Wayne were talking and Wayne offered Stuart a drink. Stuart refused but in the course of their conversation, Stuart made the statement that "It is no secret what God can do." John Wayne said, "Stuart, you ought to make a song out of what you just said!"

That night Stuart Hamblen went home and wrote these words:

"The chimes of time ring out the news another day is through.

Someone slipped and fell. Was that someone you?

You may have longed for added strength your courage to renew,

Do not feel disheartened for I have news for you:

It is no secret what God can do. What He's done for others, He'll do for you.

With arms wide open, He'll pardon you.

It is no secret what God can do!

It took him just seventeen minutes to write his song because he had lived it. He had experienced what he was saying first hand. He did not have to rely on what someone else had told him. I am not saying that the other songs are of less value because they were not experienced first hand. My point has to do with spiritual experience. When it comes to knowledge of God and other spiritual experiences, nothing can take the place of first hand experience. If it scares you to talk with someone about spiritual matters, it might be because you are trying to depend on what other people have told you as being true. You have not ventured out to find out for yourself what is true and what is not.

Perhaps you have heard your pastor say certain things but they have never become part of your own personal experience. It is hard to write a song or talk to a friend based on second hand information. So, I would encourage you to ask God to help you look again at the different facets of your faith and help you – help us all – to have a faith that we know is real because we have tried it in our own lives and found it to be true.

Prayer: Dear Father, please help us to experience Your Presence, every day, so that our faith will not be based only on what someone else has told us but that it will be based on what we know, first hand, by our own experience. Amen

CHAPTER 3: HAPPINESS IS A CHOICE

There was a song, written by a very talented young man named Bobby McFerrin, in 1988. It went like this:

"Here's a little song I wrote, you might want to sing it note by note – Don't worry, be happy!"

"Into every life there's trouble, but if you worry you make it double - Don't worry, be happy!"

It sounds kind of silly but it was number 1 on the charts for some time back then. So why would it be so popular?

I think that one of the basic needs of mankind is to be happy. But, from the very beginning we seem to think that happiness is something that happens to us. The baby comes into the world saying, "Happiness is having my milk when I want it! Wah!" That quickly progresses to having more toys, then a car, then a good job, then marriage, etc. Now, all of that is good and is part of life. But to think that happiness consists of that progression is, I believe, an error. I do not believe that happiness is something that happens to us. Happiness is a choice that we make!

Many people spend years of energy trying to find happiness from somewhere outside of themselves – a new this or a different that. Finally, if they are fortunate, they discover that happiness does not come from outside at all. It is something that you choose to be.

There is a wonderful little book, "The Way Back to Mayberry" by Joey Fann. It takes different episodes of the Andy Griffith Show and brings out sparkling teachings from the story. He talks about one episode, called "Happiness Is a Choice", when Christmas time was almost there and Andy decided to let the few prisoners that were there go home to their families "on their honor" so that he and Barney could close the jail for Christmas. But old Ben Weaver, of Weaver's Department Store, forced Andy to take another prisoner at the last minute, fouling up Andy's Christmas plans.

Andy could have had any of several reactions. He could have

gotten mad and sulked. But Andy chose to be positive. He asked Aunt Bea and others to decorate the jail and bring all of their food to the jail. He had all of the prisoners to bring their families to the jail and they had Christmas at the jail that year. Old Ben Weaver even committed a misdemeanor so that he could be "locked up"with the others. So, in the face of disappointment, Andy CHOSE to be happy. That illustrates what I mean by happiness being a choice.

In every situation that ever comes to an individual, happiness is always – ALWAYS – one of the options that are available. It might not always be an EASY option but it is always a possible choice, and, I believe, it is always the BEST choice! No matter if the situation involves pain, disappointment, financial loss, or the loss of a loved one – we are always given the privilege of choosing happiness over sorrow, remorse, anger, fear or any number of other negative reactions.

Let me mention several thoughts or attitudes that will help us choose happiness:

There is an old saying, "I had no shoes and felt sorry for myself until I met a man who had no feet". That is no longer a "far fetched" statement, for I am sure that there are several young men over at the V. A. Hospital that meet that description. But the thought is clear. When we see others who are worse off than we are, it makes it a little easier to choose to be happy, even at difficult times.

I think about the young lady who was recently in the hospital in my city. Young and athletic, she had fallen from a "zip line" and cut her leg. She had it "stitched up" but it quickly became infected with a sort of "flesh eating bacteria". Within a few days she had lost a leg, both feet, and both hands. But from the beginning she chose to be happy to be alive! She could easily have said, "Let me die! I have nothing to live for!" But instead, she chose to learn to walk on prosthetic legs and to use prosthetic hands and continue in school and in life! She chose happiness.

You can demonstrate for yourself at any time that happiness is a choice. Try this: Any time that you are feeling low, just sit down with a pencil and paper and jot down every blessing that you can think of in your life. Be thorough. Include everything. I guarantee that, before long, you will begin to feel truly happy. You have, in a sense, chosen to be happy instead of miserable. It is as simple, though not always as easy, as that!

Another way to help bring about happiness as a choice is to do something for someone else. Volunteer to drive an older person on a shopping trip. Send an extra copy of a newspaper article about a person that you know, along with your congratulations or condolences. Send some money, anonymously, to a family that is having a hard time. Become a hospice volunteer. Bake some cookies for the police or fire department. You will find happiness by your choice.

Lastly, get into the habit of always saying to yourself, any time that your happiness is threatened for any reason at all - "I can choose happiness instead of unhappiness! I can choose confidence instead of fear! I can choose love instead of hate or unconcern. I have the ability to choose my attitude in this situation!

"Help me, God, to remember that the Angels said, 'fear not' not 'try not to fear'. And help me to remember that Jesus said, 'Let not your heart be troubled'. He did not say, 'Try not to let your heart be troubled!'" A person can rightly be commanded to do something (for instance, "fear not") ONLY if he has a clear choice in the matter. The shepherds did have a clear choice the night the angels told them not to be afraid, and you and I have a clear choice when we choose happiness.

CHAPTER 4: IN THE BUNDLE OF LIFE WITH GOD

If you were to ask me what my favorite scripture in the Bible might be, I would have to say that there are two that share equally. One is 2 Cor. 5:18, 19. "And all things are of God, who hath reconciled us to himself by Jesus Christ, and hath given to us the ministry of reconciliation. ...God was in Christ, reconciling the world unto Himself...and hath committed unto us the word of reconciliation."

The other scripture is found in I Sam. 25:29. "But the soul of my lord, David, will be bound in the bundle of life with God".

Let us look at the second scripture first. It comes out of a story about David. When David was a young man, he had a small army of loyal men and they were encamped in a field next to a pasture owned by a wealthy man named Nabal. While they were camped there, the sheep and shepherds in the adjoining field were threatened several times by wild animals and David's men protected the sheep from harm by driving away the animals. This brought gratitude from the shepherds.

A little later, when David's men were running low on food, he sent a small group of his men to request just enough food to keep his men until they could replenish their supplies. Instead of being grateful and generous, Nabal sent the men away, saying, "I don't owe David anything!" Nabal's shepherds reminded him that David's men had saved his sheep on several occasions, but that did not change his attitude at all.

David was furious when he heard of Nabal's outrageous conduct, and was preparing to punish Nabal, possibly by taking his life and devastating his property. But Nabal's wife, Abigail, heard of the situation and quickly loaded a large amount of food on donkeys and sent them to David with her servants. Then she came humbly to David herself and begged for Nabal's life. She said, in effect, "Please, my lord David, overlook my husband's stupidity and greed. He is terrible but he is the only husband that I have!"

Besides the abundant food, she offered this beautiful blessing to

David. "But the soul of my lord, David will be bound in the bundle of life with God!" I will come back to that statement later.

The other scripture has to do with God's purpose of reconciling the world unto himself through the ministry of Christ and the added ministry of each of us.

Now, what does reconciliation mean here? You might think of it in terms of forgiveness, as Abigail desired for her husband, and you would be right. But I think that reconciliation goes much deeper than mere forgiveness. Can you imagine for a moment that you have had a falling out with your brother or your parents over some disagreement and the break in your relationship has gone on for years. Finally, the breach is mended with many tears and hugs. Can you imagine what that would feel like? Much warmer and deeper than mere forgiveness!

That is what God wants for every man, woman, and child in the whole world. But, even beyond that, He wants to be "In the bundle of life with us!" Do you remember hearing what it was like during the great depression? Thousands, perhaps millions of men were out of a job and many of these were "hobos" - that is, they rode the freight cars from town to town looking for any job that they could find.

These hobos would take their few precious possessions and tie them in a little bundle in a scarf or bandana. That is the picture of the "bundle of life". That is the vision that Abigail had. It is God's most precious possessions - David and you and I are among them, along with everyone else that God can get to come! And God is in their with us, for eternity!

That is what we can look forward to for the rest of eternity. Oh, not bound up in the sense of losing our freedom, but being with God and all that He has prepared for us for the rest of eternity!

Prayer: Dear Father. Help us to feel the total joy of knowing that what we have on this earth, as wonderful as it is, can not hold a candle to being bound in the bundle of life with You forever. Amen.

CHAPTER 5: MEMORIAL DAY

Memorial Day is a time when we honor our service men and women, especially those who have died in the line of duty. There have been several wars in our life time - World War II, The Korean War, The Viet Nam War, two wars in Iraq, and the war in Afghanistan.

I would like to take a few minutes this morning to remember, especially, the war of our childhood - World War II, and the men and women who served and died in that conflict.

My earliest memory of World War II was seeing my father glued to the radio late each evening in 1939, listening to the radio reports coming from Europe on the transatlantic cable.

I remember the day that Pearl Harbor was bombed. I guess every one of you remember where you were when you heard the news. My family and I were in Miami, walking down the street. As we passed an Italian Restaurant, someone ran out shouting, Pearl Harbor has been bombed! We are at war!

I remember seeing a big Liberty ship at a dock on Miami Bay and men in combat uniforms climbing the long ladders up the side of the ship - going to Europe. In another year's time we were living in Savannah, and because of the manpower shortage, my mother was a "Rosie the riveter", helping to build more Liberty ships in the ship yard at Savannah.

Our country was so unprepared for war when it started. I remember that Life Magazine showed pictures of our young recruits practicing with wooden rifles because that is all that they had in the beginning. All of our industries geared up to produce weapons and necessities for the war effort.

I remember standing in my back yard when I was in the third grade and watching hundreds of bombers and fighter planes flying out of

Hunter Field going to Europe. We often saw long convoys of army trucks and jeeps going to war.

Many things were rationed - meat, butter, sugar, gas, rubber products, shoes. Whatever was not rationed was hard to find. We had red and blue ration stamps and red and blue tokens.

Almost every family had someone in the service. My father was a sailor in the Merchant Marines. Every family had stars in their window and when one of the boys or girls were killed, a gold star went up. You probably had at least one uncle or cousin or maybe your father in the service.

The songs were so important. They played on the radio and on our 78 rpm records. There were crazy songs like, "Mairzy Doats" and "Three Little Fishes". But many of the songs were about prayer and God, and faith. There were songs like: "Praise the Lord, and Pass the Ammunition" and "Coming In On A Wing and a Prayer".

We bought Victory stamps at school and pasted them in a book that added up to a $25.00 Victory Bond that cost $18.50. We saved aluminum from gum and cigarette wrappers and took them to the movies where we deposited them in a big box in the theater lobby.

But with all of the hardships, those were very happy days! We had patriotism. We had unity of spirit as a nation. And we had hope for peace in the future. One of the songs that reflected that hope was: "The White Cliffs Of Dover"

I remember VE Day - Victory in Europe. My mother and I were staying with my aunt in Savannah at this time and our room was upstairs. I remember as if it were yesterday that we were in our upstairs room with the radio on. We were listening to what was going on in New York City. The announcer was describing the pandemonium. There were fireworks, horns honking, and sirens blaring. Then we looked out of our windows and saw that the same thing was happening all over Savannah. Everyone was just overcome by the excitement that the awful war was coming to an end.

So many boys and girls answered the call in World War II and Korea, and Viet Nam. And more recently, twice in Iraq and now in Afghanistan. We honor those soldiers, sailors, marines, air force, Wacs, Waves, and nurses. One of the things that I have been doing for about a year is when I see a soldier in a store or restaurant, if I can do it without causing a disturbance, I go up and simply say, "Thank you for serving." The response has always been a very grateful and obviously sincere "Thank you. I appreciate that, Sir!" It only takes a moment to do and perhaps it will lessen the anxiety the soldier might feel in leaving his family or concerning his or her own future safety. Now let us pray for God's continued blessing of our country and our service personnel in these difficult days.

Prayer: God, you HAVE blessed America. We would ask this morning that you continue to bless us and the whole world with peace. Please teach us how to have peace in all of the many places where there is still turmoil - even in our country, our state, and our city. Bless our boys and girls who are serving all over the world today, and help them to feel your Presence. We pray in Christ's name. Amen

CHAPTER 6: MY "DRUTHERS"

How many of you remember the comic strip, Li'l Abner? It was in all of the papers during our childhood. Written by Al Capp, it was also made into a popular Broadway Musical. Well, someone in that comic strip used a phrase - "If I had my druthers..". I know Li'l Abner used it and maybe his Mammy and Pappy did too. But it conveyed the idea that, "If it were left up to me, this is what I would choose."

Jesus used a similar phrase one night. It was after the first Lord's Supper. Judas had already gone to betray Jesus and Jesus knew it. Jesus had already warned Peter that he would betray Jesus before morning. Jesus saw His death coming closer and closer. He asked his followers to wait for Him while He went to pray. They all went to sleep! He prayed anyway and this is what He said: "O my Father, if it is possible, let this cup pass from me. Nevertheless, not as I will but as as Thou wilt."

In other words, Jesus was saying, "Father, if I had my druthers, I would prefer to go on preaching, teaching, and living in fellowship with my friends and family." But he quickly expressed an even higher "druthers". You see, even though he had an immediate personal preference, His ultimate preference was always not only to DO the will of the Father but to really PREFER whatever the Father wanted. He felt this way, not just in order to PLEASE the Father but because He truly believed that, in the words of the old television program, "Father knows best!"

For many years my "asking prayers" have tended to be rather short, because I was inclined to just say, "Whatever you want to be done about this, Lord, is what I want!" Then I began to think, "Maybe I don't care enough about things that I should care about." When others would be in anguished prayer about something, saying, "Please God, please," I would find myself saying, "Whatever You think is best, Father." I began to question if I was just being uncommitted to the outcome, like the husband who says to his wife, "whatever!" But then there came a time when I was tested and I learned the truth.

It was when my son, Dean, was in an automobile accident in Miami. As an aftermath of that accident he faced a crucial time in the hospital and was very close to death. On the morning when the results could have gone either way, I got up before sunrise and went to my favorite spot on the beach. There, as the sun came up over the water, I met God in prayer. With Dean's life at stake, I asked that, if possible, his life might be spared. But I knew beyond any doubt that I wanted God's will more than I wanted mine. I was not trying to please God with my attitude. I sincerely believed with all of my mind and heart and soul that His will was really best for my son and for my wife, and for me. On that morning, alone on that sunlit beach, I placed my son's life into the arms of God. I knew that he was safe no matter what happened. I knew that my manner of prayer from that day forward would be to state briefly what I would prefer but then to desire with all my heart that God would do whatever was best!

I think that, perhaps, God wants us to state what our druthers are for our own good. Do you remember that, sometimes, Jesus would ask someone that He was about to heal – like the blind man - "What do you want of me?" Jesus already knew what he wanted. He just wanted the man to be sure that HE knew what he REALLY wanted. I think that is the way God wants us to pray. Tell God what we want of him so that WE will know and then turn it over to the Father because He always has the very best outcome in mind. This kind of praying - which, after all, is Christ's kind of praying – is not just giving deference to God. It is recognizing that the Father always has the best answer on any issue – any issue!

I believe that praying in this fashion shows that we are moving from being spiritually immature towards being spiritually more mature. So, whether we are praying about what kind of car to buy or we are placing the life of our loved one into God's hands, we would be wise to do as Jesus did - "Father, if it be possible, then here is what I would like. But, nevertheless, not my will but thine be done!"

CHAPTER 7: MY PERSONAL ASSESSMENT TOOL

Most businesses have some sort of assessment tool or formula that they use to tell where they are in relation to where they want to be in the future, what problems they might have in reaching their goals, and how they might prepare for the problems that they anticipate.

I think that it might be helpful if individuals had a similar tool that they could use at significant points in their lives, such as at the beginning of adolescence, the start of young adulthood, middle age, and where some of us are now - "The mellow, senior years"!

Such a tool for the Christian might be something like this:

Ask God to help you see clearly where you are this very moment in relation to what He would like for you to be.

Ask God to help you see two things clearly. What you would really like to do and become during your remaining years on earth , and secondly, is that what God wants?

Ask God to show you any problems that might keep those desires for your future from happening.

Lastly, ask God to show you what He would suggest about meeting these problems successfully.

I would like to show you how this might work by describing three hypothetical cases of people much like you and me.

First is Laura. Laura is 79 years old and is a widow. God has shown her that she is living in a wonderful space right now. She still drives, even on long trips by herself. She has minimal health problems and is in regular touch with her daughter, who lives in the same town and her son who lives about 200 miles away. Laura feels good about her relationship with God, and is active in her church. She feels that God is pleased with the way she is "behaving herself"!

The possible problems that she anticipates are both health related.

She is afraid that she might lose her health to the degree that she can no longer drive or live independently in her own home. She has worried about these two possibilities a great deal.

During several times of prayer, Laura has felt the following insights from God: "Laura, barring sudden death, like a heart attack, you WILL experience loss of health that WILL, sooner or later, keep you from driving and living in your own home, unless someone comes to live with you. It is not IF but WHEN. You can depend on this! It is just the normal result of aging. But I will be with you each step of your aging process. I will also be with each person who is in any way effected by your aging process. In the mean time you can enjoy giving your full effort into living each day to its fullness and doing all that your hand finds to do. Then I will welcome you back to my Presence when your time comes. Laura, just remember, all is well!"

Next is Jim. Jim is an 80 year old gentleman who is happily married and is actively networking on the computer. He is active in his church and is a teacher in the ESL program there. It is his desire to learn conversational Spanish. There is a large population of Hispanics in his city and he wants to be a volunteer missionary in their community. He is enrolled in a basic Spanish class at the local college and also in a conversational Spanish class.

The only problem that he sees in his future is the possibility of his dying before he can realize his plan. He would like to serve as a volunteer missionary at least several years if his health permits.

Jim has prayed about this and has gained an assurance from his prayers that this is a calling from God. God has convinced him that he needs to redirect his concern from how long he can serve to the more appropriate issue of continuing to faithfully prepare himself and leave the time table to God. He does not worry any more about how long he will get to serve, or even if he will actually get to serve actively as a volunteer missionary in the formal sense. God has shown him that he is already a missionary in language training and will remain so as long as God desires. In other words, Jim has arrived at a place in life in which he has no desire to do anything beyond the time that God wants him to do it. Jim, and also his wife are trying to live every day at God's beck and call. They also believe that all is well!

The last example is Doris. Doris is an active church member. She is 85 years old, teaches an adult Sunday School class, is in the choir, and is the oldest adult worker in the childrens' Seekers Program on Wednesday evenings. She wants to continue all three of these activities as long as possible.

Doris has begun to have a few "senior moments" and can not remember names as easily as she once could. This has begun to worry her and she fears that she is in the beginning stage of getting Alzheimer's disease or some other form of dementia. She fears that this might cause her to give up one or all of these activities.

God has calmed her fears somewhat, as He did with Laura, by assuring her, through a book that she has been reading about Alzheimer's, that two things are true. First of all, that it is not a matter of IF she will eventually have to give up an active leadership in those activities but WHEN. She is seeing that it is only being realistic to see that her interest will some day have to be reduced to prayer and encouragement from the sidelines. But, secondly, the slowing down of her mental acuity and the lessened ability to recall names as readily as before does not in any way necessarily mean that dementia is on her doorstep. She can easily have several years of active enjoyment ahead.

Lastly, God has reassured her that, when her time does come, He will take her to be with Him and she will not miss anything from her earth experience in the slightest. There will be someone ready, prepared by God, to take over her Sunday School class, her group of Seekers, and her alto part in the choir. Her children, grandchildren, and great grandchildren will always keep her in their hearts. She is now convinced that all things are working out just as God planned and all is well! It really is!

Prayer: Dear Father. Help us to always keep in mind, whatever our age, that our stay here on earth was never meant to be permanent. That we are here to accomplish certain things and then come back to you. Help us to always feel, each minute of our lives, that all is working out according to Your plan and that all really is well. In Christ's name, Amen

CHAPTER 8: SMALL WORLD *

Most of us have had at least one incident in our lives that has caused us to use the expression, "Well, it's a small world after all!" I can remember three such happenings in my own life and I would like to share them with you.

When I was eight years old I attended the third grade at 38th Street Elementary School in Savannah, Georgia. I have a group picture of that class, taken on the front porch of that school in 1942. I treasure that picture, of course. Forty years later I was working as a chaplain in a hospital in Augusta, Georgia. In one of the units I saw someone who looked vaguely familiar. I doubted that I could have known this person before and after all I often see people that I think I have known before and it seldom turns out to be so. But the feeling persisted so I approached the man and saw an identification tag that identified him as Dr. Benfleld.

I said "Dr. Benfleld, I am Bob Ringwald and I can't help feeling that I know you from somewhere, did you ever live in Savannah?"

"Why, yes, in fact I grew up in Savannah."

"What schools did you attend there, Dr. Benfleld?"

"Well, I went to 38th Street School."

"Well, so did I. Were you in Mrs. Hager's third grade?"

"Yes, I was."

"Are you Daryl Benfleld?" "Yes, I am!"

"Daryl, you haven't changed a bit. The other night I was looking at a picture of that class and you are standing right next to me and we're both wearing short pants!"

"Hey!, I'd love to see that!"

"I'll bring it tomorrow!"

"Wow! It's a small world!"

When I was 9 years old I was surprised one day to hear my name on the radio. I heard this very melodious voice saying, "This is Bob Ringwald, speaking to you from New York and this is the Columbia Broadcasting System.. "Wow", I said, "there's somebody with the same name as me and he's talking on the radio all the way from New York". After that, whenever someone would ask me my name they would say, "Bob Ringwald, just like the radio announcer?" And I would proudly say, "yep, same name!"

About forty four years later, in the same hospital in Augusta, there was a reorganization and I, as Chief Chaplain was placed in a Department of Coordinators with the Head of the Physical Therapy Department. His name happened to be, yes, you guessed it, Bob Ringwald. We would get each other's mail and enjoyed other confusions from our identical names.

One day I said, "You know, Bob, until I met you I had never met anyone else with the same name as mine, although I was proud to know that there was a radio announcer with the Columbia Broadcasting System in New York named Bob Ringwald. Do you remember hearing him when you were a boy?"

"Well, yes, I heard him every day. He was my father!"

"Wow, It sure is a small world!"

When I was in high school in Jacksonville, Florida, I was in the band, and it was the center of my social life. In fact, it meant so much to me that I have kept up with the members of the band and of my class of 1951 through Joe Hampton, who is a sort of email coordinator of all that goes on in our lives. He came across an old band picture, taken on the field during a halftime show. There were several of us prominent in the photo - three trombone players and two majorettes in the center. He sent the photo to me.

Weeks later I was enjoying an outdoor cookout and was talking with a gentleman who was very knowledgeable concerning rock and roll groups. He mentioned that the Lynard Skynard Band came from Robert E. Lee High School. I said, "You mean Robert E. Lee in Jacksonville, Florida?"

"Yes, are you familiar with that school?"

I said, "Yes, I went there for three years!"

"Well, did you know Mary Slater and Don Slater?"

"Well, sure, Don was a great football player and Mary was the head majorette in the band and I played trombone. I marched right behind her!"

"Well, Mary was my first wife".

"You don't mean it. Where does she live now?"

"Right here in Augusta. I can give you her phone number!" Well I called her when I got home and we had a great reunion. I said, "Mary, I am looking at a picture right now. We are on the football field and you and I are no more than three feet apart."

"Yes, I think that was the night that we did a routine when they turned all the lights out and I sang, 'Just a Song At Twilight'. We each even had a little flashlight on our cap."

"Yes, I can see the little flashlight on top of each of us. How about that!" "That was fifty seven years ago and two hundred miles from here!" "Now, where do you live in Augusta, Mary?"

"I live on Merrimac and Caulfield, Bob, where do you live?"

"You won't believe this, Mary, but I live less than a mile from you!"

"Wow, It really is a very small world, isn't it?"

All of these illustrations remind us that we do live in a very small world. Several of the astronauts have commented on how the world reminds them of a small boat that all of us are in together. I heard the story about three pirates whose ship had been sunk in a battle. The three had survived by getting in a small rowboat together. As they were taking turns rowing toward a distant shore, one of the pirates became angry and shot the third. The remaining pirate said, "Why in the world did you do that?"

"He said something that I didn't like!" was the answer.

"But there was only three of us to row and now there are only two!"

The same is true of all of us in the world today. We are all in a relatively small boat in space. It behooves us to take care of our boat and of one another. Anything that we do to harm each other harms us all. Anything that we do that harms our earth is harming the only boat that we possess!

*Names were changed to protect privacy.

CHAPTER 9: STORIES FROM OUR ESL (ENGLISH AS A SECOND LANGUAGE) CLASS

My wife and I taught an ESL class(English as a Second Language) for 14 years. During that time we came across a number of interesting stories from our students. I would like to share just a few of those this morning and perhaps present some others at a later time.

There was a young lady from China, who used the American name, Amanda. She shared with us that she had never seen anyone hugged in her native China. It was not a practice among her family or anyone that she knew.

When she came to ESL class, her teacher (in another class) hugged her. She said that it made her feel loved. When she went home that day, she hugged her husband. He said, "Are you crazy?" She said, "No, but the lady who teaches me in ESL hugged me and I liked it, so I thought I would hug you." When she hugged her daughter, later in the day, her daughter thought something was wrong with her. She explained why she did it and the daughter still was not sold on the idea. But the next time she hugged her husband and daughter, they seemed to like it.

It gradually became a practice in her family, but someone had to demonstrate it by their own actions. The teacher showed one way that love is expressed.

There are people in the world who have never heard of a God of love and are just as surprised the first time they hear about the God that we have known about all of our lives. All that they know is a god of fear or vengeance or jealousy or hate. We can demonstrate God's love just as simply as that teacher demonstrated love to that Chinese girl. When we show kindness and consideration and understanding in our everyday lives, it demonstrates to others what our God is like. There are people from all over the world right here in Augusta. We have a mission field right here in our own back yard.

There was a young officer from the nation of Slovenia, which was once part of Yugoslavia. His name was Ales and his wife was Mateya. They had a young son. Ales was an officer in the Slovenian Coast Guard and he was temporarily studying at Fort Gordon. The country's small Coast Guard had about three small boats. Ales said that Slovenia had two young men studying at the United States Air Force Academy. He said that when the two men graduated, they would be the Slovenian Air Force!

We had Ales and Mateya and their son over to our house for dinner one evening. They were amazed that we had four bedrooms. They said that they had just one bedroom in their apartment in Slovenia. They said that only rich people were able to have two bedrooms. They could not believe the fact that we had meat, several vegetables, and a dessert. They said that their typical evening meal consisted of a stew made from whatever they had in the refrigerator.

The comparison between their life style and ours made us very grateful that we live in a country like the USA. It also made us aware that we really ARE rich. We are rich compared to the way that much of the world lives today. We are also rich because we have a knowledge of God that much of the world does NOT have.

Another student, Mary, was from Brazil. She was here for several years because her husband was in a training period as an employee of a large Corporation.

Mary came to class crying one day. She shared with us that, in her country, she was a pharmacist and owned a pharmacy which employed several dozen people. Here she had nothing to do and she felt so useless!

After class I took her over to the children's building and introduced her to the Director of the Children's Program. I explained the situation and the Director put her to work immediately, taking care of children. First as a volunteer and then as a paid worker. She worked in that capacity until she went back to Brazil. She said, "Rev. Hancock, you are an Angel sent from God!" I think God just used the information that I had already to bring joy into Mary's life. Yes, in that sense I guess I was an Angel sent from God. After all, the angels in the Bible were just messengers sent from God. God can use you in that same way in the course of your day if you will ask Him to do so.

There was another young lady from Brazil, named Nathalia. She was a journalist in her country. She came to our class and was very bright. One day she told me that she was Catholic but that she heard our choir on television one Sunday morning. She said that she loved to sing and wished that she could sing in a choir like ours. I said, "then come this Wednesday evening! I will meet you and take you to choir and introduce you to our Choir Director!" She DID come and, though she still attended her own church on Sunday, she practiced every Wednesday night with our choir and sang at our Christmas Programs for two years before she moved away!

There are many people who are introduced to our church through our television ministry. If we keep our ears open, we will hear them make a comment about hearing our service and it can open the conversation to an invitation to attend our church, to talk with one of our ministers, or to share some need with us as a friend.

The last example that I would like to share is a friendship. It was a friendship between a lady from Israel and a lady from Lebanon. Not only were they friends but they were Best Friends! They were supposed to be enemies! Their countries were at war during those days. But they simply did not accept the idea of "enemy".

It seems to be a common human trait that we must always paint our "enemies" as evil. When we were children in the 1940's we readily accepted the idea that the Germans and the "Japs" were evil. I guess that is part of what it takes for a nation to get its young men ready to shoot the enemy.

But, after the war, we found that the German and Japanese people are just people like us! We sit with a German lady every Wednesday night who spent her childhood listening to our bombs! She was a child over there while I was a child over here! After the Korean war we found the same to be true of the Korean people! After the Viet Nam war - the same!

Now we are going through a period in which it would be very easy to put all of the Muslim people into one group that we might suspect are potential killers, terrorists, or Christian haters. Yet, in ESL we have known some very sweet, loving Muslim people who are much more like us than they are different.

What this says to me is that people all over the world are just people. Some operate out of love, some from selfishness, some, even from hate. But they are all just people. Rather than labeling them "enemies" or "friends" according to their race, nationality, religion, or politics, why don't we try to see each person on the basis of how he demonstrates his own character?

I often said in ESL, "We, in this room, are like the United Nations! Yet we have such love and respect for each other! If it was left up to us there would never be another war!"

Isn't it interesting that every nation that we have ever had a war with or been hostile with have also been our friends at some time or other? As someone once said, "Wouldn't it be nice if some day they had a war and no one came?"

Prayer: "Dear Father, help us to show your love in everything that we do and help us to be more like you, being more interested in making friends than enemies. In Christ's name, Amen."

CHAPTER 10: THE CHURCH THAT GOD MOVED

I read about this event in Paul Harvey's "The Rest of the Story", and it was so astonishing that I had to seek further authentication. I went to my computer and found several sources that said it was well documented.

In 1874, members of the Methodist faith in Swan Quarter, North Carolina, decided to establish a permanent church building. A committee of the group picked out a very desirable location in the heart of town, but the owner of the property would not sell to them.

They settled on a parcel of land that was donated to them in a less desirable location, in back of the present Court House.

In 1876, the following series of events took place. On September 16, on the eve of the dedication of the church, a tremendous storm, with strong winds and rains, took place. The water rose to such heights that it floated the wooden frame church off of its brick foundation. The church began to float down what is now called Oyster Creek Road. Many people came out with lengths of rope to try to tie it off to posts on the way, but were unable to do so.

It moved down the road until it bumped into a general store at a corner of the road. It then took an abrupt right turn and proceeded down that road for two blocks until it reached what is now called Church Street. It then took a left turn, crossed a canal, and settled in the middle of a field owned by Sam Sadler. It happened to be the very site that had been refused to them originally! When the owner saw what had happened, he decided that it was, indeed, an act of God, and he delivered the deed to the field to the minister of the church. Years later, the church was renamed "Providence".

In 1912 – 13, a new church was built and the old building was sold to a farmer, to be used as a barn. In 1940, the old building was purchased and given to the Providence United Methodist Church – the church that had been built in 1912 – 13. It was renovated and stands on the site that it occupied when it was first built. It was divided into a fellowship hall, Sunday School classrooms, and a kitchen.*

This seems to have been a well documented event, and the people involved seem to have accepted it as an act of God. It is certainly possible to see this and similar events in history as being simply fascinating examples of coincidence. But, to me, it is one more building block in my faith in a God that, on occasion, takes an active part in history. I can be as much of a "doubting Thomas" as anyone and I do not accept such anecdotal stories lightly by any means. But when something like this comes with eye witnesses who were properly interviewed on a first hand basis, it seems to support such happenings that are called "miracles" in the Bible. It does tend to strengthen my faith in the God of the Bible. I hope that it will do the same for you.

It is my understanding that a visitor can retrace the travels of the church and also see the original church and the newer church called Providence United Methodist. It seems to me that such a visit might be a nice day trip for a family!

- My computer information was gleaned from: "Ancestrally Challenged" and can be found on the computer at "The Church moved by the hand of God."

CHAPTER 11: THE SINS OF OUR FATHERS

In the Bible, Exodus 34:7 and elsewhere, it says that God visits the sins of the fathers on their children and grand children. If we look at the story of the exodus of the Hebrews from Egypt, we see this in operation to some degree.

God had told Moses to lead His people to the promised land. In a very short time, after the exodus, many new things had taken place - the people were organized into tribes, a traveling tabernacle, or place of worship, had been built, laws were passed, a priesthood was established, and they arrived at the doorway of the promised land. All was ready!

They sent spies into the promised land, including Joshua and Caleb and ten other men. Joshua and Caleb reported that it was a wonderful land, flowing with milk and honey, and that they could win against the people there. But the other ten men said that the people there were like giants and that they would not have a chance at all to take the land.

The outcome was that the fathers of the tribes believed the ten men with the negative report. They turned and ran back to the desert. As a result, the Hebrews wandered in the wilderness for 40 years. Probably no one over the age of 20 at the time of that decision, ever set foot into the promised land except Joshua and Caleb. The children of these men must have often said, "If only our fathers had been brave and wise we would be enjoying nice homes and schools and normal lives by now, instead of wandering around in the desert!"

Did you ever have similar thoughts about your parents? Do you think your children ever had similar thoughts about you? Did you ever feel that your father was too strict? That you missed some really good times because your parents were too protective? That your life might have been different if they had just let you do this or that? Are there things your father did or did not do or say that makes it hard, even now, for you to forgive them for? If you were able to choose a different father now would you want him to be like Joshua and Caleb or like the other ten men? Which group was your own father like?

Any time you hear sermons about the 40 years in the desert, it is usually about a negative event. The fathers were not brave and courageous. They did not trust God. Therefore they "suffered" for 40 years in the wilderness.

But now, let me put a little different perspective on the wandering. These men meant well. They probably had the welfare of their wives and children foremost in their minds. The outcome of the 40 years was not necessarily bad. All of the laws, rituals, organization, etc. had time to mature and develop. The people built a history and a spirit of unity. They were probably much better prepared, in many ways, to enter the promised land than they would have been before. What I am saying is, that just maybe the decision of the fathers was really a good thing!

In my own case, much of my childhood was spent with a single parent – my mother. She made some decisions that I felt, at the time, were mistakes. I felt bad about some of those decisions. For instance, when I was in the first grade we lived in Port St. Joe, Florida. It was a very happy time in my life. It was secure, I had many friends, good school, many happy play days, a seemingly happy home. Then, it seemed to me for no good reason, my mother took me and left my step father. I cried every night for a very long time. Over the next 8 years, before I was even in the 10th grade, I had moved 10 times! There were times when I felt that my mother was making big mistakes!

But, looking back on my life, I realize that, first of all she was doing the best that she could. Even more importantly, I believe that those seeming mistakes were the very things that made me who I am today. I would even say that I am a better person because of the experiences that came out of those seeming mistakes. I can even thank God that those mistakes took place. Just as the Hebrew children might have felt when they looked back on their 40 years in the desert.

How about you? Can you see that your father, your parents, did the best that they could? Can you appreciate that those things that your parents did or did not do, that you considered mistakes, were the very things that made you the person you are today? Can you accept the idea that the things that you might have considered mistakes with your own children were the very things that made them what they are?

So the decisions made by parents are not so much good or bad as they are the stuff that our lives are made of. And I truly believe that God uses all of those decisions, just as they are, to build our lives as He wants them to be. Not perfect by any means, but human and meaningful and good!

So, as we approach this Fathers' Day, let us thank God for our fathers – our parents – and for their decisions – good and bad – that formed who we are today.

Prayer: "Dear Father. We thank You for our fathers, for our mothers. We thank You for trusting us to be the parents of our children. Most of all, Father, we thank You that the decisions and actions of our fathers did not have to be perfect in order for You to use them for good. In Christ's name. Amen"

CHAPTER 12: THE VALUE OF A PERSON

Imagine that I have a bag. I pull out two bills from the bag – a one dollar bill and a one hundred dollar bill. These two bills are the same size, have about the same amount of ink, weigh the same. What makes one of them 100 times more valuable than the other? The value is not in the material but in the value that people agree to place upon them.

Then, suppose I pull out a gold ring or a diamond stone. In that case the value is found in the material itself, especially because it is scarce.

Still again, what if I bring out a hammer, a screw driver, and a pair of pliers. These are not valued by the value that people have agreed to place upon them or by the material that they are made of. They are valued, primarily, by how well they fulfill their purpose, how well they do the job they were designed to do.

The value of human beings is based on all three of the above! Let me elaborate.

We are valuable because of the value placed upon us by God, by our loved ones, by our friends, and by ourselves. The Bible tells us that God created us in His own image and then He called his creation "good". I certainly hope that your own family experience has convinced you that they and your friends value you, though I am sure that there are a great many unhappy people in the world today who had a different experience from that. But such a negative experience does not take away from your true value.

Secondly, we are like gold and diamonds, in that we are valuable because of our scarcity. There is only one person like us in the whole wide world. There will NEVER be another person like us. If there was only one Panda bear or one Labrador Retriever left in the whole world, can you imagine how valuable it would be? There is just one of you and one of me!

Lastly, we are valuable because of the purposes that we fulfill. Just as a hammer has a specific purpose that can not be served by a screw driver, you and I came to earth to fulfill some very definite purposes. I know that there are things that we do that someone else could do just as well or better. But there are other specific things that God has sent us here to do that no one else CAN do. We touch people in ways that ONLY we can do. We do this day in and day out! We do it just by being ourselves.

This value does not cease when we are no longer young or employed or thinking clearly. Nor will it cease when we are no longer on earth, for we will continue to be valuable in the memories that people have of us. Even more important than that, we will still continue to exist and remain a value because we will be in some other part of the universe still!

Who are you? You are not primarily a physical being who came to live 70 or 80 years on earth and then die. You are a spiritual being who was created to live eternally. You have come to live a few years on earth to learn and to grow and carry out God's purpose on earth in the fashion that one might be blessed to go and enjoy Germany or France for a number of years as a representative of a company or a government. Then we would return to those that we represent. We simply represent God and Heaven! We are, indeed, very valuable!

CHAPTER 13: THINGS MY MOTHER TAUGHT ME

As you know, you learn a lot in elementary school but you also pick up a lot of good things from your parents along the way. Some of this I have to laugh about in retrospect. I hope it will also be funny and familiar to you. But I do not mean any disrespect, for my parents were young and times were difficult. They shared what they had learned from their parents.

To begin with, as far as medicines were concerned, the following rules applied. All cuts and abrasions got an immediate application of iodine. The fact that it hurt meant that it was killing germs. Twice a year, spring and fall, we got a big dose of mineral oil. We also got a glass of orange juice with the mineral oil, to cut the taste, but it only ended up making me hate the taste of orange juice for years. A number of stomach ailments got castor oil, also with orange juice. Other stomach ailments got a general cleaning from Black Draught – a black powder that totally cleaned your system.

There were a number of "don'ts". "Never eat the bottom tip of an ice cream cone. You don't know what might have fallen down in there!" "Never eat fish and drink milk at the same time." I was in college before I took a chance on that. I was quite surprised that I did not get sick. "Never swallow a water melon seed. A water melon might grow in your stomach." "Never swallow a fish bone, you might bleed to death inside." I still get filet fish whenever possible. "Always cut off the little tip end of a banana ." I still don't know the reason for that. I guess it just doesn't look good. Anyway, I always do it.

"Always blow through a soda straw before putting it into a drink." That was before the day when straws were individually wrapped. They were just open in a straw holder. "Never drink from a soda bottle that has a chip out of the rim. The chip might be down in the soda!" "Always tell the barber to leave your side burns!" "Never go roller skating in your good pants!" I did roller skate one Sunday afternoon in my new Shark skin pants and fell down, making a hole in the knee. I went to bed with a sprained hand and was awake all night, rather than tell my mother. I went to the doctor the next day!

We were constantly told that we would get "ground itch" if we went barefooted but they let us go barefooted anyway. AND we got ground itch anyway! "Never look 'cross eyed', Your eyes might lock up!" "Don't 'make faces' at people. Your face might freeze that way!"

Along with all of the above, I learned to be kind to other people. I learned that family always help family and neighbors always help neighbors. I learned that there is no hurt that a hug and a kiss won't make feel better.

I learned that even a 12 year old could get a social security card and get a job in a grocery store if he wanted to. And I did!

Only two times do I remember my mother getting real mad at me. I am sure there were others but I do not remember them. The first time was when I was six years old. I walked up town to our regular grocery store and "charged" a bag of bananas without my mother's permission. I thought that if you "charged"something that it was free. She taught me the difference! The other time was also when I was six and in the first grade. The teacher caught me writing spelling words on my desk before a test. I really did not know how bad a thing that was. But I sure knew that night. My parents took me that very night to meet Mrs. Gunn, my teacher, at the school. No spanking was necessary and I don't think I ever tried to cheat on a test again from that day 'til this.

My mother taught me how to say my first public prayer. I had been asked to lead in prayer one night at church training union when I was 12 years old, and it scared me to death. I asked her how to do it and she wrote down what to include in a proper public prayer.

I learned that God loves me and that becoming a Christian was a good thing. About six of us in our extended family, including my mother, got baptized on the same morning in the same water!

My mother taught me that, if I wanted to do something badly enough and God wanted me to do it, that we would find a way to do it somehow. I wanted to go to military school in the 9th grade. She helped me get together the $20.00 I needed to buy a used uniform. I wanted to go to college and we found a way, year by year. We never had any doubts that I would finish!

When I left home to be on my own, I had no doubt that my family loved me, that God loved me, and that the world was a wonderful place to be. I feel so blessed to have grown up in the 40's and 50's and to have had a mother who probably never finished high school, since she was married at age 15, but who knew enough to teach me everything I needed to know to get a good start.

Prayer: Let us pray. "Father, thank you for letting us grow up when we did. It was a good time for kids! Thank you for our parents and for our extended families. Thank you for all the things that we learned from them. Amen"

CHAPTER 14: THREE KINDS OF FAITH

Have you ever had someone come up to your front door with a sad story, like, "I'm on my way to my brother's funeral in Wrens and I gave out of gas, could you..." I have. So, picture this next scenario for a moment. You notice, through your front window, that a fellow is coming up the street, he eyes your house, picks up a rock out of the street, and rings your doorbell. You reluctantly open the door, knowing that your screen is locked. He says, "Pardon me, Sir. Excuse me for bothering you. My wife is very sick and I am trying to raise enough money to pay for her medicine.

One of my prize possessions is this genuine piece of the old Berlin Wall. I would never consider selling it if it wasn't for my wife being sick, but I am trying to sell it for just $10.00. Would you like to buy it to help me out?" You know that it is a rock he just picked up from the street! I am pretty sure I know what your answer would be!

Now, let me tell you about another rock. It really IS a piece of the Berlin Wall! At least I believe it is. It says so on the label. My son bought it for me from someone that he trusts! It has notarized documentation. I really believe that it is authentic. But I do not know this beyond all doubt. I have to depend on faith.

Lastly, let me picture another scenario. Imagine that you happened to be in Berlin on vacation during 1990, when the Berlin Wall was actually being torn down. You are standing there in amazement as the pieces are flying here and there. You see some of the rocks fall near your feet. You look around and there is nobody saying that you can not pick some of them up. So you stuff your pocket with enough to give a historic souvenir to your friends and family back home.

Now I have used these three representations of the Berlin Wall to illustrate three kinds of faith.

The first rock, picked up from the street and offered as the "real thing", represents every source of false hope that mankind has ever settled for – alcohol, drugs, physical attractiveness, money, fame –

many other things that people have put their faith in to bring them lasting happiness. It is faith but it is misguided faith and it will fail.

The second rock is the Gospel about God that we have heard in good faith and accepted as truth on the basis of our trust in the Sunday School teacher, preacher, parent, friend, and Bible. We do not absolutely know that it is true. We must accept it on faith because we have not actually seen Christ or experienced Him bodily. We certainly HOPE that it is true and we base our lives on it being true. Our faith is usually strengthened over time as we experience God's working in our lives. But it is still based on what someone else has told us.

The third rock – the one we saw fall from the Berlin Wall with our very own eyes - represents the kind of faith that Thomas experienced AFTER Christ showed him His hands and side. It is the kind of faith that Peter, James, and John had AFTER seeing the resurrected Christ and AFTER experiencing the miracles of Pentecost. It is the kind of faith that a select few have experienced from special "signs" that God has given since that day – like to Saul on the road to Damascus and to John Wesley and a few others that we read about in the history of the church.

That third kind of faith is what I have often wished for. It is a faith that is more like actually knowing than hoping. But instead I am "stuck", like many of us, with the second kind of faith – the kind of faith that has to depend on what someone has told us. I say "stuck" because I would much rather have that stronger kind of faith, like Paul and the disciples had. But you know, God has recently shown me a scripture that I have seen many times before but never taken to heart. It is the conversation between Jesus and Thomas when Jesus said, "Thomas, you have believed because you have seen my hands and my side. But blessed are those who have not seen and yet have believed."

To me, God is saying, "Don't fret, Donald. Your faith is the harder kind! Anybody can have faith when they are knocked down in the road and blinded, like the Apostle, Paul. But it takes a greater faith to believe when you have NOT had a special sign. Jesus called you 'blessed'! Be content with that!" And, I am trying!

Prayer: "Dear Father. I would still like to have a stronger faith. I would still enjoy getting some sort of strong sign from You. But please help me to learn to be content with the faith that I have, if that is your will. In Christ's name, Amen."

CHAPTER 15: WHAT DO WE HEAR?

A Cherokee Indian was visiting his friend in New York City and they were walking down one of the busy streets when the Indian paused and said, "I hear a cricket!"

"You're kidding me, right?" said the friend.

"No, I really hear a cricket."

The friend said, "Man, there are cars, taxis with horns blasting, people walking, talking. You can't possibly hear a cricket!"

The Indian stopped, looked around, then walked to a small plant in a cement box. He lifted a leaf and picked up – a cricket. "How did you do that?" said the friend.

"My ears are different from your ears," said the Indian, "I am used to hearing crickets. You are not. Watch this." He took a handful of change from his pocket and dropped it on the sidewalk. Dozens of people all around them stopped, turned, and checked their own pockets. "That is what you are used to hearing," said the Indian.

That story made me think about our own hearing. What do we hear from each other? For instance, what do we hear from our church staff? We hear our pastor's jovial voice as it carries over the noise in our fellowship hall. But do we hear in his voice perhaps a bit of discouragement on a Sunday when attendance is unusually low or when he senses that his sermon did not quite make the grade?

We are used to hearing the cheerfulness of our children's worker when she tells the children a story on Sunday morning. But do we hear her disappointment when a well planned program turns out a smaller than hoped for response from the church members? Well, yes. I think we do at least sense those things, but maybe we do not know what to say. May I make a few suggestions?

When you hear in their voice or spirit something like, "I really am trying to do my best for the church and for God, but...", just take a moment to say, "You are really doing a good job!" Be generous in your words. "That was pretty good" never helped anyone! Saying nothing would be better than "pretty good."

When possible, on Sunday morning, instead of going right out to your car, take a few moments to comment to the choir director that the choir special really helped you worship this morning. Perhaps say to the pianist or organist that their solo during the offering was especially good today. If you see a choir member on the way to your car, comment to her. Such words cost you nothing but can be very affirming to someone who has worked hard to do a good job.

If you see a custodian, tell him that you appreciate how clean and neat everything looks. Call up the secretaries sometime just to tell them that you appreciate all the work that they do. Take a moment on Wednesday evening to thank the kitchen volunteers and workers.

Now, how about when you hear something in a friend's voice – discouragement, tiredness, sadness, or maybe joy? Why not say, "You look like you might be feeling a little "down" today – what's going on?" or "You sure are smiling this morning, did you get some good news?" Then listen and respond with interest, understanding, sympathy, encouragement, or whatever is appropriate.

Perhaps just your listening is all that they need. But if you are not listening then you will not hear at all. You might just miss a great chance to be of help!

What do you hear in the grocery store or department store? First of all, I have discovered an unusual phenomenon. As you hurry into a department store and you notice someone coming in back of you, holding the door for them works a small miracle every time! During that short moment I hear racial barriers falling and generation gaps narrowing and gender gaps giving way to gentleman like civility. When you hear a young man, who looks pretty rough, say, "Thank you, Sir" or "Thank you Ma'am," I think that is a beautiful moment!

Just a smile at the girl at the register in the grocery store and a sympathetic word, like, "Has it been a hard day?" or "You really look chipper today!" according to what you hear from their body language, can make their day easier.

I have said this before but it warrants repeating – When you see a soldier in the aisle of a grocery store or in line at a restaurant or just wherever he or she might be, all you have to say is, "Thank you for serving!". You will hear heart felt gratitude. I have never heard otherwise. You might just lighten their anxiety about leaving their family or their own future safety. That is well worth taking a few moments to do.

What do you hear from your own family? Do you hear the enthusiasm or the impatience or the yearning for independence from your granddaughter? Take time to respond to what you are hearing, even if it is just a word or two. At least they will know that you are hearing them. What about grandchildren, nieces or nephews going to college or starting a family? Hear their fears and joys and respond as needed. They probably value your words far more than you realize.

Believe me, it is possible to be around all of these feelings and miss hearing them as surely as the New Yorker missed hearing the cricket. But, on the other hand, you can listen and be sensitive and furnish a ministry of encouragement that can continue as long as you have life and breath. Remember that Jesus said when you minister in that way to others you are also ministering to Him.

I would like to paraphrase part of the prayer of St. Francis of Assisi and let that be both a guideline for our hearing and also our prayer this morning. Let us pray:

"Lord, make us instruments of Thy peace -

Where I hear discouragement let me speak encouragement.

Where I hear injury let me speak comfort.

Where I hear doubt let me speak acceptance and faith.

Where I hear despair let me speak hope.

Where I hear darkness let me speak of light.

And Where I hear sadness let me speak joy!In Christ's name, Amen".

CHAPTER 16: A MUSICAL MIRACLE

Last Thursday night I saw a musical miracle. At least it would seem like a miracle to the ears and eyes of a layman. But it was actually a testimony to the musical talent of hundreds of dedicated musicians who, with a minimum of practice time, put together a concert that ranged from the simplest "Jesus Loves Me" and "Praise God From All Blessings flow" to the most magnificent grand opera quality presentation of "The Midnight Cry".

This concert was presented in Augusta, Georgia by four separate groups that came together for one seamless presentation that gave the impression that they had worked together forever. One group was a men's group, called the Sons of Jubal. This group consists of Church Musicians from all over the state of Georgia. A comparable women's group, The Jubalheirs, is made up of volunteers, female Ministers of Music, and some of the wives of the Sons of Jubal. (The name, Jubal, came from the first musical person mentioned in the Bible, in Gen. 4: 21.) Then there was a brass ensemble and a separate orchestra ensemble, both of which consist of Church Musicians from Georgia. The fact that they could even make a presentation with no apparent error after minimal practice together is like a miracle within itself. But to present such a magnificent performance was a double miracle!

There were probably over 300 in the combined choirs, but it was the orchestra of over 50 musicians that held my attention for most of the evening, perhaps because I have played trombone in our own church orchestra. This group had the clarinets, oboes, English horns, etc. in the reeds. There were the violins, violas, cellos, and just two bass viols in the strings. In the brass there were many trumpets, French horns, euphoniums, TEN trombones, and one Tuba. In the versatile percussion section there was a man and two women who literally played everything that will shake, rattle, or resonate to a drumstick, plus a drummer who manned a set of drums the whole evening. Then there was a piano, organ, and several fine conductors. There you have it. But why would I choose to tell about this in a devotional piece? Let me share with you what I experienced.

Actually, the choral group, as marvelous as they were, were mostly just the background for me. The main focus of my attention was on the orchestra the whole evening. Now the singing was important, of course, for without the singing the message would not have been as clear. But my eyes and ears were constantly on the orchestra! Surprisingly, much of the orchestra itself was background to what I watched most consistently. My head movement was somewhat similar to that of a tennis match as it ranged primarily from the two bass viols on the far left, to the solo Tuba and three of the percussionists on the far right, with an occasional look in on the drummer who sat at a set of drums in the center, just in front of the conductor. Now why would I, with so much to see and hear, concentrate so consistently on seven of these many fine musicians? Let me share with you the "why"!

The first reason is, there must be something in my musical DNA that makes me love the deep bass undertones of any music. Perhaps it is because I began my musical training with a tuba and then settled in on the trombone. But when I hear music of any kind, while most people are hearing primarily the melody, in my head I am processing the bass foundation of the piece. But that, in itself is not enough to cause me to share this experience in a devotional thought.

The second reason is that these seven players especially, along with the rest of the orchestra, represent to me the people that we see, every day, in our lives. Let me explain:

The orchestra as a whole, represents the organized society in which we live, each member of our environment doing his own part of what it takes for us to live our good life. They do their "thing", rest, then do it again – all under the direction of the laws and elected officials who keep us straight – our society's conductor. Or, you could think of the orchestra as being all of Christian society, under the direction of God. Or, to make it even more personal, think of the orchestra as our own local church.

In our church we each apply the talents that God has given us. We play our part and rest. Then we play our part again. Our conductor is God, but He often delegates His directing to many others including the ministers and elected leaders. Some of these leaders

45

are like that drummer with the drum set, known for doing their special thing and doing it well.

Other leaders are the multitaskers, doing many things unnoticed, behind the scenes. Let me refer again to the percussionists on the right end of the orchestra. One would be playing the tympani drums. He would keep his eye on the music and his drumsticks on ready for measure after measure and then strike his drums three to five times, stop, then watch his music for measure after measure with his drumsticks on ready. Just three to five strikes on his drums, but each strike so very, very important. Then, there was a lady playing a small xylophone type of instrument for a while. Then she would stop, reach over and strike a cymbal two or three times. Then back to the xylophone - all of the time watching her music - much of the time just waiting and ready. Another lady might be playing a rhythm instrument that few people would even notice, but it added its little rattle that made the song just right.

Now there are so many of you that are like those percussionists. You add a little bit here and a little bit there – cooking a meal, making a visit, writing a letter or email, saying an encouraging word. You are versatile but often behind the scenes. You probably often wonder if what you do amounts to anything. It does! After the concert I could hardly wait to tell the percussionists how much their work had enhanced my enjoyment of the music. I think they were genuinely surprised that anyone had noticed. But they did appreciate it. I was very sincere in saying that. You who add your own touches behind the scenes need to know that about yourselves too!

Also, I noticed that the percussionists worked together as a team and communicated as they worked. I would see the man playing the tympani whisper to the girl playing a rhythm gourd and they would switch places. I could imagine that the conversation went something like this, "There's a tambourine coming up in 5 measures, would you do the tympani while I do that?" That is what happened anyway. That is not unlike some of your conversations when one of you call another to see if she can do a dessert for the lunch for the family at a funeral tomorrow and the second lady says, "I can do the dessert in the morning but I have a dental appointment at 11. Can you possibly pick it up and take it?" "Sure, Thanks" Your work is often behind the scenes and few people know about it. But it enhances the enjoyment of many, including God.

Now, about the bass sound. I also went up and told the bass viol players how much their bass chords meant to me. They also seemed surprised and appreciative. (I looked for the tuba player but he was gone. To me the bass is usually simple, perhaps even boring to some. They do not usually have a lot of fast runs or solo parts. But the slow, almost syrupy tones add foundation and body to what is happening in the melody above. All music would lose a great deal if we had to depend just on the instruments with a higher range. The truth is, we need ALL of the instruments in every register to make the music rich. What does this say about you and me? Well, some folks seem like solo type instruments by nature, with abilities that amaze us. We would be greatly hampered without them. But others of us are happy to be in the background, supporting the others with prayer, interest, and just "being there". You represent to me the tone of the bass viol and the tuba. You are every bit as valuable to society, to the church, and to God.

I am so grateful that I went to that concert. I hope that the comments that the experience inspired in me will encourage you to see how very valuable you are, no matter what your experience, talents, personality, and position might offer to the music that God is making through all of us.

CHAPTER 17: DOING WHAT IS RIGHT – REWARD OR NOT
This is reported as a true story and I have not been able to verify or find it to be false. It does have a worthwhile moral.

In 1892, a young 18 year old was struggling to pay his college fees at Stanford University. He and a friend came up with an idea of how they might raise some money for their education. They would bring a musical concert to the campus, see to all of the details themselves, and have enough profit, after expenses, to cover their unpaid college fees.

They decided to approach a pianist by the name of Ignacy Paderewski, a Polish musician who had already gained world fame as a pianist. Paderewski's manager said that he could only come to Stanford if the boys could guarantee his fee of $2000 for the concert. They stepped out in faith and made an agreement. They worked hard to make the concert a success. But to their chagrin the total sales amounted to only $1600.

They went to Mr. Paderewski and explained the situation. They gave him the entire $1600 and a check for the balance. They promised to make the check good as soon as they could. Mr. Paderewski surprised them by giving the money back and telling them that he would take only what was left over after they subtracted their expenses and what they needed to pay off their college fees.

This was a very generous thing to do and the two young men never forgot his kindness. The young men went on to their respective careers and Mr. Paderewski went back to Poland and eventually became the Prime Minister of that country.

When World War I came to Europe, Poland was devastated. There were over a million people starving in that country. Mr. Paderewski did not know where to turn. He reached out to the United States Food and Relief Administration for help. The head of that agency was Mr. Herbert Hoover, who later became the United States president. Mr. Hoover immediately sent tons of food to Poland for their relief.

Mr. Paderewski was so grateful that he decided to go to America immediately and thank Mr. Hoover personally. When he began to thank Herbert Hoover, Mr. Hoover quickly stopped him and said, "You should not be thanking me, Mr. Prime Minister. You may not remember me, but several years ago, you helped two young students go through college at Stanford University. I was one of those two students!"

There are other examples of this happening in history. Most of us remember the fable of Androcles, who took a thorn out of a lion's paw and the lion later saved Androcles from certain death. That, of course, is just a fictional teaching story, but it teaches that good deeds of compassion will ultimately be rewarded. But we should not do good deeds just because they might be rewarded. Mr. Paderewski did not do what he did for reward but because of his compassion for the boys and because he saw it as the right thing to do.

The Bible points out that very teaching in a scripture found in Ecclesiastes 11:6 - "In the morning sow thy seed, and in the evening, keep on sowing. For you do not know which seeds will grow and which will perish. So keep on sowing!"

I heard the same idea expressed by a professor that I had in the seminary. "When you go out to fish, you do not know where the fish are biting. So it is best to fish in every pond that you come to!"

So, whether the idea is, help an animal that is hurt without expecting any reward, as with Androcles, or sow seed consistently because you have no way of knowing which seed will grow and which will not, or fish in every place where the opportunity presents itself because there is no way to know where the fish will bite and where they will not – all of these old sayings are basically saying, "Do good every time you have an opportunity to do so. Sometimes you will be surprised with a reward and often you will not. But keep on doing good wherever you can anyway!"

Mr. Paderewski did not expect a reward. He was just a kind and fair man who saw the opportunity to help those boys. He probably would never have considered doing otherwise. But this was one of those examples when God saw to it that the "lion had a chance to repay Androcles", and when the seed did grow up over time and rewarded the one who had sown consistently both in the morning and in the evening. So, let us do likewise. Let us always be ready to help each other whenever the Lord gives us an opportunity to do so. Let the reward of knowing that we helped be reward enough. Sometimes there might be even some extra reward added on!

Let us pray: "Dear Father, thank you for every opportunity that you give us to do something good for someone. Help us to do it without thought of reward. Then, when we are surprised with some reward, help us to be genuinely grateful. In Christ's name. Amen."

CHAPTER 18: FAMOUS PEOPLE WHO FAILED BEFORE THEY SUCCEEDED*

This particular article would possibly be more appropriate for young people just starting out in their careers, but instead it is being prepared as a devotional piece for a group of senior adults, many of whom are in the 70 to 90 year old range. So why do I think that it might be inspirational to them?

First of all, people of that generation (which is also my generation) are still trying to achieve in many different areas in their daily life. In that striving to accomplish, they still meet times of defeat. I have found that, even at my age – 79 – it still gives me a morale boost to know that people like Winston Church failed many times before achieving success even after they were in their middle 60's. So, the theme of this devotional will be, "Take heart, all of these folks failed big time before they made it!"

HENRY FORD: All of us have grown up thinking of Henry Ford as the man who practically invented the concept of the assembly line. His motor company is one of the oldest and most substantial businesses in America. But we must not forget that he made five attempts at business and each one left him totally broke before he founded his successful auto business!

F.W. WOOLWORTH: We also grew up longing for Saturday, when we would get to go to town and browse through the "Dime Store". We would look up and see those big gold letters on the red background and feel such a sense of awe. What a super achiever Mr. Woolworth must have been! But before he started his own business, he worked in a dry goods store and was not even allowed to wait on customers because his boss did not feel that he had the sense needed to do so!

COLONEL SANDERS: The king of fried chicken is known throughout the world, along with Coca Cola and McDonalds. But his famous "secret chicken recipe" was turned down over 1000 times before the first restaurant accepted it!

ALBERT EINSTEIN: If someone were to mention the word,

"genius", perhaps the person who would pop into your mind would be Albert Einstein. But he did not show any promise at all early in his life. He did not speak until he was four years old. He did not read until he was seven, causing his teachers and his parents to think that he was mentally handicapped and antisocial. Eventually he was expelled from school. But, at some point, he caught on and, in the end, won the Nobel Prize and changed the whole direction of modern physics.

THOMAS EDISON: I guess we have all heard that Thomas Edison made 1000 unsuccessful attempts to perfect the light bulb before he found the right combination. But did you know that, in his early years, his teachers told Edison that he was "too stupid to learn anything" and that he was fired from his first two jobs for not being productive enough.

WINSTON CHURCHILL: Winston Church stood almost as tall to us, in our childhood, as our own President Roosevelt. But, though he was elected Prime Minister of England twice, he did very poorly in his early years. He struggled in school and failed the sixth grade. In his political life he seemed to be a perpetual failure, losing every election for public office until he was finally elected to Prime Minister at the age of 62.

ABRAHAM LINCOLN: Abraham Lincoln had a similar pattern of failure. In his youth he went to war a captain and returned as a private. He started numerous failed businesses and was defeated in many elections for public office before finally becoming President.

OPRAH WINFREY: Oprah Winfrey is well known today as one of the best known women in television, but did you know that she was once fired from her job as television reporter because she was considered "unfit for T.V."

FRED ASTAIRE: I think that I have mentioned before that the man who was the dancing idol of everyone in our childhood years had the following note pinned on his first screen test by the testing Director of MGM: "Can't act, can't sing, slightly bald, can dance a little."

SIDNEY POITIER: One of the highest regarded actors in the business and the winner of an Academy Award, was told by the casting director, after his first audition - "Why don't you stop wasting people's time and go out and become a dishwasher or something?"

J.K. ROWLING: J.K. Rowling is well known today as the author of the very popular Harry Potter book series, but before she wrote the series she was a single mother, severely depressed, living on welfare, nearly penniless, attending school and trying to write a novel. She went from living on welfare to being one of the richest women in the world in a 5 year span through hard work and determination.

ELVIS PRESLEY: As one of the best selling artists of all time, Elvis has become a household name, even years after his death. But when he began, in 1954, he was fired by Jimmy Denny, the manager of the Grand Ole Opry, after just one performance, and told, "You ain't goin' nowhere, son. You ought to go back to drivin' a truck!"

Now, all of these famous folks must have had times when they were down in the dumps and thought that their lives were going nowhere. Most of them, by their own admission, had some degree of faith in God and depended on Him. What I hope is that seeing the contrast in the lives of these folks, before and after, that we might have a moment in which we can feel better about those times when we also feel down. May we be reminded that the rich and famous are just folks like ourselves. Their notoriety puts them in the news but God is just as much available to us as He is to the richest and most famous. Our work is just as important to God as theirs is.

- This information came from the following Internet site: http://superforce101.wordpress.com/2010/04/20/50-famous-and-successful-people-who-failed-at-first-succes s-secrets/

CHAPTER 19: GOD CAN BLESS THE CHANGES IN YOUR LIFE

My early life, up until my high school years, was touched by constant change. I had ten different school changes before I got to the tenth grade. It would seem that such changes, and the nature of those changes, would have been bad for me. But, as I look back on my life, it is very apparent that God used those changes to bring me ever closer to Himself and to His plans for my life. I would like to share, briefly, how that worked. I hope that this will help you to see His working in your own life as well.

I was born to a young couple in Savannah, Georgia. I do not know my father's age but my mother was 15 when she married and 16 when I was born. It was during the depression – 1933. Neither had a church background. Those were difficult times and jobs were hard to find. The marriage dissolved when I was three and my mother remarried within the year. We moved to Callahan, Florida, and then to Port St. Joe, Florida, following job opportunities.

My step father was very good to me and gave me many lessons and skills that would benefit me even until today. For the next four years, through the first grade, I had a wonderful life. If you can picture Opie's early life, on the Andy Griffith Show – that was me. Neighborhood kids to play with – rubber guns, kites, catching tadpoles, walking to school.

Only once was I ever in church. There was a revival at First Baptist Church of Port St. Joe and we attended one night. I spent the evening in the nursery – I was about 4 years old – and it made no impression on me, other than it was the first time that I had seen the inside of a church. I can see the sanctuary in my mind's eye even now. I do not remember having any impressions about God at this point. But I am sure God was working.

At the end of my first grade in school, my mother left my step father. I felt bad about this because I was very happy with my life. We went to Miami, where my father had a sign shop. He was a sign painter by trade. I believe my mother had hopes of reconciliation, but it did not happen. For much of the next few years I lived in a single parent home. I was in Miami for a full year, and I attended the second grade there. God used this time to develop a longing in my heart for Him.

Every Monday morning my elementary school would have an assembly and the Principal would ask, "how many of you went to church yesterday?" Many of the kids got to raise their hands but I never could. There was a Baptist Church within sight of my house and it is still there. I longed for someone to ask me to go there, but it never happened. It was no one's fault. I guess it had to be that way for me to develop the desire to know God. I could have gone by myself. I walked to the movie theater by myself and it was many blocks further away than the church. I was not afraid of the trip. I was uncertain of what it would be like inside of the church. But God was preparing me for what would come next.

At the beginning of the third grade my mother and I went back to Savannah and lived for a while with my Uncle, Aunt, and three cousins. God was ready to introduce me to what church was like. My cousins went to Sunday School and I went with them. At first it scared me. We would sit around an oval shaped table and one of the activities was to read the Bible around the table, with each boy reading several verses. I did not read very well and often felt embarrassed. Then we would all go "up to church" and hear the sermon. I remember complaining that "I didn't understand the big words that the preacher used!" But we still went every Sunday to Calvary Baptist Church. I attended Sunday School, Training Union, Church, Choir, Royal Ambassadors, and Boy Scouts there through the ninth grade, with the exception of a year that I was in New York. I will say more about that later.

While at Calvary I became a Christian and God used those wonderful days to mold my character and to prepare me to be willing to answer His call when it would come later on. My extended family, especially my cousins and my paternal Grandmother and Grandfather, would fill in many gaps that would have been there if it had been just my mother and me alone.

I mentioned my year in New York. My mother and I lived in the small town of Mechanicville, New York during the year that I was in the seventh grade. God used that time to broaden my horizons. I attended an American Baptist Church and my best friend, Paul, was the son of the Pastor there. I made many friends (this Georgia boy was something of an oddity up there) and I thoroughly enjoyed the winter of sledding, ice skating, and living in an entirely different setting.

In the eighth and ninth grades I was back in Savannah and, again, attending Calvary Baptist Church. In the ninth grade I attended Benedictine Military School. I enjoyed the uniforms, the R.O.T.C. Military discipline, and being in the band. God used that time again to broaden my horizons. I gained an appreciation of the Catholic Brothers and Priests who were my teachers. My parents moved to Jacksonville, Florida before the school year ended but they arranged for me to stay at the Catholic Boys Home that was affiliated with the school. God again used that time for me to experience a different way of worshiping Him. The boys would get up every morning at 5:30, go to breakfast, do assigned chores, and then attend Mass. I learned the "Hail Mary" and many of the other Catholic worship forms while I was there.

When I went to Jacksonville in the tenth through senior years of school, I was truly ready for God to work with me in preparation for his call to the ministry. High school and the band was half of my social life. Riverside Baptist Church was the other half. During those years I sang in the choir, attended every activity in my age group, and became the Royal Ambassador Leader while in my Junior year of high school. One day one of my teachers, who was also a member of my church, asked me what I felt God wanted me to do when I finished school. For the first time I expressed to another person that I thought maybe God wanted me to be a Minister. God firmed up that calling and led me to go on to Stetson University and Southern Seminary.

Yes, my early life was subject to many changes. But God used every one of those changes to bring me always closer to Him and to His plans for my life. Looking back I could not have possibly chosen a happier or more rewarding childhood. I thank God, my family, and all of the other people that God placed in my life, for keeping me safe, happy, and on track for who I am today.

Prayer: "Thank you God, for being with me all of those years, and for doing the same with each of these folks who have read these words today. Amen."

CHAPTER 20: HELP WAS THERE*

Yoni was an Israeli Defense soldier. He was at his guard position in Hebron when he was shot by an Arab terrorist. It was early in the morning and it seemed, at first, that no one else heard the shot. The soldier fainted from the trauma and was bleeding profusely. He would have died very shortly. But another soldier did hear the shot and was able to locate Yoni and stop the flow of blood. He held his hand over the wound until someone else came and summoned help.

Yoni was taken to a hospital in Beér Sheva and his life was saved. His parents were called to the hospital and were so grateful for his safety and that his life had been saved by the quick action of his fellow soldier. They asked where the other soldier was and the hospital staff said that the other soldier had left the hospital when he knew that Yoni was out of danger.

Although Yoni's parents were relieved that their son was safe, they somehow felt that the story was incomplete because they had not been able to thank the unknown soldier. They went to the military to find out who else was serving in the area that morning but they were unable to find out anything.

The mother knew that the important thing was that her son was safe. But she could not seem to get it out of her mind that she needed to thank the other soldier. She finally thought of a plan. The parents ran a little grocery store in Kiryat Malachi – a town near Ashkelon. Since Israel is a small country and many people move through their area, they would post a sign outside their little store and they would explain briefly on the sign just what happened with their son and state their desire to meet the young man who had saved Yoni.

Nothing happened for almost a year, but finally, one morning a customer read the sign and recalled that her son, Yair, had been involved in such a situation a year before and how happy he had been because he had obviously saved his fellow soldier's life. The lady went into the store and told her story to the delight of Yoni's mother. The mothers both called their sons on cell phones and they were able to arrange a meeting that very afternoon with both families attending.

There was much joy and happiness as the story was told and details were filled in. During the tearful conversations, Yair's mother called Yoni's mother aside and they went outside for privacy. Yair's mother said, "You do not recognize me, do you?"

"I am sorry to say that I do not," answered the first mother.

"There was a reason that I was at your store this morning," said Yair's mother. "I was in town and I wanted to come by your store and thank you for something that you and your husband did for me twenty years ago. Do you remember a young girl who came into your store and had a sad story about being pregnant?"

"Of course, Dear. I remember now! You were considering having an abortion."

"Yes, and you and your husband were able to encourage me to go on and have the baby. You assured me that God would help me through the trials of rearing the child and that some day I would be very glad that I had made that decision."

"That is right," returned Yoni's mother.

"Well, not only 'some day' would I be glad that I had my baby, but from the very beginning, the moment that I held my Yair, I was glad!"

"Then Yair was the baby that you chose to have!"

"Yes!"

"And because you chose to have your child, my son was saved?"

"Yes!"

"So I am doubly thankful for that day, twenty years ago, when you made your decision and we were able to help you!"

The two women hugged and shared their joy over the way that God had worked out His providence on their behalf.

Now, this story speaks strongly on behalf of those who discourage abortion. But I realize that many folks believe very sincerely on both sides of this issue. What I would like to bring out in the story of Yoni is that God, in His providence, arranged, twenty years before the event, for two young men to both be alive and in the same place when they were needed - Yair, to be the rescuer, and Yoni, to be the one saved. Both were brought together at just the right time to complete the story that had made a twenty year pilgrimage to bring back together two families and to show them the correctness of a scared young girl's decision so many years ago.

It is my conviction that God is doing such things much more often than we realize. If we could see all of our individual life histories the way God does, I believe that we would see God's "finger prints" on countless bits and pieces of each of our stories. But only a few of these stories make the newspapers.

Let us pray: "Dear Father, thank you for not only creating us but for participating actively in each of our lives day by day. We thank you for walking with us each day and sometimes even touching us in special ways in order to bless us. In Christ's name, Amen."

*The facts for this story can be found at the following site:
http://www.friendsofefrat.org/idf-story.php

CHAPTER 21: LIVING IN TWO MODES – FEAR AND NON – FEAR

I would like to share two experiences that I have had – about 70 years apart – that, I believe, illustrate two modes of living..

The first experience was when I was in the second grade, living in Miami, Florida. I was what might be called a semi-latch key kid. Both of my parents worked at night in their small family business. It was just a few blocks away and I felt fairly safe. At night I would finish my home work, listen to the radio for a while, and then go to bed by myself. On this particular night I turned out the light and pulled the sheet up over me. A few seconds later I felt someone sit on the bed. I was petrified! I could hardly breathe out of fear. I was totally still for at least ten minutes, afraid to move. I had never felt more fear in my whole life.

But finally, I got up the courage to turn on the light and face whoever was there. There was absolutely no one else in the room. I got back in bed, but this time I left the light on. As before, I pulled the sheet up over my body. But this time, I noticed that the sheet billowed up, full of air like a parachute. It took several seconds for the material to settle down on the bed and on my body. Again, it felt just like someone was sitting down on the bed. So, all of that fear was understandable and yet absolutely unnecessary. I was never in any danger at all. But I had lived through those long minutes thinking that I was in great danger. It is my belief that many people live their whole life in such a fear mode as that!

The second experience is one that I am currently having, and enjoying, on a regular basis. I have a flight simulator on my computer. With this simulator I can choose one of about twenty different airplanes and fly out of hundreds of airports all over the world, sitting at my computer. I take off and land as safely as possible. I obey all of the rules of flying. But, if I make a mistake or use poor judgment, I can crash just as surely as if I were flying a real airplane. Yet, it is a "simulated"crash. There is a flash, an explosion, noise, and a demolished airplane. But there is absolutely no pain, except to my sense of not having had a safe flight. The airplane and the pilot return immediately to the runway to take off again. There is NO REAL DANGER EVER! Now, again, I always fly as safely as I know how, as though my life depended on it. But it NEVER does. I am NEVER in danger, and I KNOW it.

Now, let me review. In the first situation, I thought that I had good reason to be afraid, but I didn't. From the limited perspective of the darkened room I had reason to think that I was in great danger. But when light was brought into the situation, it was quite clear that there was no danger at any time. In fact, in retrospect the situation was laughable.

In the second situation, in order to enjoy the flying experience, I did everything as though my life depended on my skill and the dependability of the airplane and the environment. But in reality it did not! It NEVER did! I make each flight with a complete absence of fear! Of course!

That brings me to the topic of this devotional – living life in two modes – fear and non fear.

I feel that God intends for each of us to obey certain rules in life, symbolized by such traditional wisdom as "don't touch a hot stove or jump off of a building over three feet high". But I do not believe that we need to go through life trembling when we are near a stove or when we are required to go up in an elevator. Such fears would be unreasonable. It is my personal belief that all of the dangers that we encounter in this life are, in reality, like the danger that I imagined in my childhood experience. I do not mean that they do not exist in reality but that they do not offer any ULTIMATE danger.

Let me explain. We tend to worry about many things that effect our lives, sickness, death, losing a loved one, losing our job, not having enough resources for our old age, failure, making mistakes. But these things and many more are not ULTIMATE concerns. At best these experiences furnish the brick and mortar out of which our lives are built and made rich. These are the happenings that give us personal growth while we walk through our lives on earth. At worse, they are temporary and God will help us bear them while they last. But those of us who believe in God consider that our life on earth, as wonderful as it is, is a mere stepping stone toward what is going to be our ultimate existence – eternal life in God's presence.

With all of this said, I believe that we can live in a life mode, similar to the experience on the flight simulator, in which we will live life according to the very best that we know, following the rules, walking as safely as we know how, as though our very lives depended on US and that all of the outcomes of life were here and now. But at all times we are aware that all crashes are just learning experiences and are neither fatal (in the ultimate sense) or permanent.

As we mature in life, it is hoped that darkness is gradually replaced by light and that the dark perspective of fear is being replaced by an enlightened perspective that all is really well and that no danger is ultimately real or lasting. May you find yourself shifting from the mode of fear into the mode of non fear. May you begin to see that all crashes are simply ways of teaching us how to "fly"more safely next time. May we all hear the truth in the old Gospel song, "This world is not my home, I'm just a passin' through!"

CHAPTER 22: MUSIC IN MY LIFE

You and I are complex personalities with many facets. We are spiritual, mental, and emotional in nature, but even beyond that we have many areas of interest, talent, and environmental differences that make us the individuals that we are. Many people, over the course of our lives, have made their contributions to who we are.

Most of you know that music has been an important part of my life. I would like to share with you some of the people who contributed to this one facet of my life. I believe that you will see my purpose for this by the time I am through.

The first music that I can remember was hearing Tommy Dorsey play his theme song, "I'm getting sentimental over you". I am sure that I was only three years old because I can still see the room in my grandmothers house and hear the radio just as it was then, and we moved from that house when I was three.

Within the next several years I remember my mother singing to me such popular songs as "Pennies From Heaven" and "My Blue Heaven". My father also sang to me but it was always the same song, "Nights are long, since you went away, I think about you all through the day, My Buddy...". I am still touched every time I hear that song.

When I was in the second grade in Central Elementary School in Miami, my teacher brought out the rhythm band instruments and we accompanied a recording of "The Washington Post March". I played the sticks. We gave a concert for our parents. It was the very first time I played an instrument in a group.

When I was in the third grade at 38th Street School in Savannah, our teacher introduced us to "The Nutcracker Suite" by Tchaikovsky. She gave us crayons and rough manila paper and we drew pictures of "The Waltz of the Flowers" and "The Dance of the Sugar Plum Fairy" as those pieces were played. That began my long romance with classical music.

In the fourth grade I remember hearing a violin played in a live concert for the first time and it made tears come to my eyes. I remember telling an adult cousin that I wanted to do that some day and she said, "Maybe you can!" Those three words gave me hope.

In the fifth grade we had the only really pretty teacher I ever had. All of the boys had a crush on her. But what I really remember is that she had a piano in the class room and we did a lot of singing. One song that I remember in particular was "Cielito Lindo". This was my first experience of singing in a group.

Also in the fifth grade, my older cousin's girl friend, Niki, talked me into joining her in a tap dancing class. (Dancer Gene Kelly was popular then). I still have the program from our dance recital that year. Niki went on to dance with the Radio City (New York) Rocketts. I, well I still remember some of the steps to my recital number!

In the seventh grade I lived in New York. I joined the middle school band and learned to play the Sousaphone. That is the tuba that wraps around you. It was all brass and weighed almost as much as I did. I was allowed to take it home on week ends – wrapped around me while I walked the eight or ten blocks to my home in the snow and ice.

In the ninth grade I was introduced to the trombone in the Benedictine Military School band in Savannah. The band director was Mr. Verehees. While I was officially in the beginner band in the seventh grade, I was actually just learning to play. This experience in the ninth grade was my first experience of playing with others in an actual marching band.

In the tenth grade I was in the Robert E. Lee High School band in Jacksonville. The director was Mr. Hulik. The band was so much a part of my life that I had perfect attendance throughout high school and had no idea of that until graduation. I simply did not want to miss school for any reason!

My choir director and organist at church was Mr. Edward Bryan. Whenever he played the magnificent Bach Toccata and Fugue in D Minor he would always ask me to turn pages for him because he knew that I loved that piece.

When I went to college, I was in the band and glee club.

When I became a pastor I was often the song leader and choir director too.

When I came to Augusta as chaplain at Gracewood State School and Hospital, I was also the choir director.

When we came to First Baptist, I sang in the choir and played in the orchestra. Now I have the privilege of leading the singing in our Sunday School Department every Sunday!

Now, what is the point in giving you so much detail? It is just this. Look how many people contributed to just this one facet of my life, and that is not all of them! They never knew, at the time, that they were making such a contribution to my life that I would remember them 60 or 70 years later. Most of them are dead now and I believe that one of the joys of Heaven is being able to get a full report of the impact that our lives have made on other people. So, I believe that each person that I have named has already enjoyed knowing what their contribution has meant to me.

Now my point to you is this. Though your contribution may or may not have been in the area of music, you have definitely added your ten minutes here and your thirty minutes there to hundreds, perhaps even thousands of people whom your lives have touched over the years. And those people, if they had the privilege of standing before a group as I have this morning, would be citing what you did for them in the third grade or the fifth grade or when they were new on a job or when they were just married or new in the neighborhood or had just come to First Baptist Church.

You are not through yet! You will be making unknown

contributions to others until your very last breath. Then you will have the joy of finding out, in wonderful detail, just who and how many people your words and attitudes and actions have touched in a helpful way over the years. So please know that your life is very important to other people and has always been so! Keep doing what you are doing, knowing that God knows just how to use your words and your actions to bless other folks!

CHAPTER 23: MY FRIEND TED

A famous poem by Kahlil Gibran, says that our children are like arrows and you and I are like the bow that these arrows are sent out from. God is the archer who bends the bow to send our children on their way. Gibran goes on to say that, though they are our children, they do not belong to us. Though we can give them our love, we can not make them take our thoughts. We may house their bodies but we can not house their souls.

This morning on Mothers' day, I want to say that our children are like that and so are our loved ones and our friends. We can love them. We can try to influence them. We can pray for them. But, in the last analysis, our children, our loved ones, and our friends must choose their own way and we must release them to God's care. So it was with a friend of mine named Ted.

On a hot day in July, 1932, Ted Crawford was born. His mother must have had some jokes from her friends, such as, "Are you sure you are not carrying quadruplets?" Ted was probably a big baby. He was a big toddler - big all the way through school. He must have been bigger than his daddy by the time he was in the second grade!

Ted's mother must have spent many sleepless nights and his doctor must have worried too. You see, Ted had acromegaly, a disease which effects the pituitary gland. Everything in Ted's body grew larger than normal. But mothers can only do so much. At some point they must let their child go and hope for the best.

By the time Ted Crawford was in high school, he was 6' 9" tall - that is about one inch taller than a typical door frame in a home. He was a basketball coach's dream. Indeed, he was a gifted football player and basketball player.

By the time I got to know him, he was playing basketball and football at Stetson, my college! Ted was very intelligent, in fact I will brag a little and say that he and I set the curve in Mrs. Lowry's English Lit class - we competed for the A plus on tests and essay papers. But that is where our competition ended.

Ted majored in speech and drama. He was in plays and variety shows - he was full of talent. He would come over to our dormitory some nights (we only had about 8 guys in our dorm), and he would entertain us by improvising one act plays and comedies. I still remember one called "Wings Over Brussel Sprouts". Ted was a smart, funny guy!

In a strange, indirect sort of way, Ted is almost related to my church, First Baptist Church of Augusta. That is stretching the facts a bit but follow this. In 1955, our senior year, my pastor at First Baptist Church in Deland (where Stetson is located and many of our students attended) was Rev. James Stertz. He was my pastor there but he was my Associate Pastor here the year my wife and I joined. Well, Rev. Stertz invited a young evangelist to preach our revival. He was a former basketball player at Baylor who had also been on the US Olympic basketball team that won the Olympics shortly before that. His name was Jack Robinson, who later became pastor here at First Baptist Church.

I was very impressed with the preaching and tried to get Ted to go, but to no avail. I prayed for him and have often wondered if Ted ever developed a conscious relationship to God, but, as Ted's mother knew concerning his physical condition, all you can do is pray and hope for the best!

Well, Ted married a girl from Stetson when he graduated. They moved to Dallas, Texas, and I lost track of them for a while. I later found out that he became a popular radio disk jockey and then got involved in movies and television. It was then that Ted became my claim to fame. In all of my adult ministry, any time I wanted to impress a group of kids all I had to do was tell them that I went to school with Lurch, the butler on the Addams Family TV show. For my friend, Ted, was Ted Crawford Cassidy, alias Lurch, the Addams Family butler. YOU RANG?

As I watched Ted in movies and television over the years, I sometimes wondered if he found a relationship with God. I wondered if I said enough. Could I have said more? Sadly, I heard the announcement on television in January of 1979, that Ted Cassidy had died at age 47, of complications following heart surgery.

We, as parents and as family members and as friends, must remember that, all that we can do with our children, our loved ones, and our friends, is use our influence as best we know how, pray, and leave the rest to God. For we are the bow, our children and loved ones are the arrows, but God is the all knowing Archer.

Prayer: "Dear Father, help us to feel comfortable with our parenting, for we have sought to be the kind of parents to our children and friends to our friends that You would be pleased with. Amen."

HAPTER 24: SMALL WORLD REVISITED

I have another devotional, in this book, entitled "Small World". But I did not get to say all that I had to say and so I must go back there again. We often use the phrase, "Small world!" when we meet someone who knows someone that we know or has lived where we have lived, etc. This piece is about that type of thing that has happened to all of us.

My wife and I went on a cruise a year or so ago to celebrate our anniversary. The night that we got on the ship I prayed that God would lead us to meet people that He might especially want us to meet for whatever reason that he might have. I believe that He did that several times during the period that we were on the boat. As an example, the very next morning after my prayer, we went to breakfast and sat at a long table that had at least ten people seated. The couple right across from us were an illustration of what I would call the "Small World" experience. I will change names throughout this piece to protect the privacy of these folks.

After we sat down, we introduced ourselves to the couple across from us. "Hello, we're the Jones – Ron and Anita."

Mr. Smith: "We are the Smiths, Don and Doris. Where are you folks from?"

Me: "We are from Augusta, Georgia".

Mr. Smith: "Oh, I was stationed at Fort Gordon in Augusta for a while!"

Me: "Where are you from originally?"

Mr. Smith: "I am from Jeffersonville, Indiana."

Me: "Oh! My first job after we got married was in Jeffersonville! I was in Seminary in Louisville, just across the river."

Mr. Smith: "I took my basic training not too far from Louisville – at Fort Knox."

Me: "My first church was right down the road from Fort Knox – at Guston, Kentucky."

Mr. Smith: "Where are you from, Ron?"

Me: "I'm from Savannah, Georgia."

Mrs. Smith: "We had our honeymoon in Savannah!"

Me: "Where are you from, Anita?"

Mrs. Smith: "I am from Orlando, Florida, originally."

Me: "Oh! I went to college near Orlando, at Stetson."

Mrs. Smith: "Well, it's a small world, isn't it?"

Well, that is the way the conversation went all morning. It just seemed to say over and over again, just what a small world we live in.

I find similar unusual "tie ins" when it comes to the church that I attend, First Baptist Church of Augusta, Georgia. I was in the church choir for quite a while and one of the choir members at my church also sang with me in the Glee Club at Stetson, 58 years ago. We are now living, probably, 400 miles from Stetson. Strange that we both found our way to the same church so far from our college! Another member of the same choir went to the same elementary school that I did in Savannah, Georgia, 250 miles away from here. That was over 65 years ago. The Associate Pastor at this church, when I joined in 1986, was my former pastor at Stetson, 32 years before that. Another church member, who is also a local television announcer, went to the same high school that I attended in Jacksonville, Florida – AND attended the same church that I attended.

Another church member, who was also in our church orchestra with me, discovered that I was the Associate Pastor of a church in his neighborhood in Louisville, Kentucky, when he was in high school. He used to play basketball at the basketball court in back of the church during that period. Another church member was a Teacher Intern at a child guidance clinic in Louisville, Kentucky – the very year after my wife had held the same position. A former pastor of this church, where I am now a member, was in the Seminary with me and we were good friends. In fact, we were both pastors in the same Association while we were in the Seminary. His church was the closest church to mine. All of these were people in this one church who were associated with me years before and miles away.

As you will see, if you read my other article entitled "Small World", there were quite a few of these unusual "tie ins" that I also discovered after coming to Augusta, Georgia in 1970. I am still trying to make some sense out of what these "tie ins" indicate about the world that we live in. You, the reader, have probably wondered the same thing. I have a theory that might at least touch on what is behind this phenomenon. It certainly does not explain it but perhaps it is a beginning.

My theory is that each of us comes to earth as a member of a sort of extended family or a "drama troupe". As such, we agree before we are born to be a part of each other's life story and to play our supporting parts in each other's drama. This might explain how so many people come out of our past to touch our lives again and again.

It would also make sense if there is some connection between many of us simply because we are all distant cousins. If creation was from one man and one woman – Adam and Eve – then we are, indeed, distant cousins. If I meet someone who has the name, Collins, my mother's maiden name, I just must ask them about their roots. If they happen to be from anywhere near Statesboro, Georgia, then I must let them know that we must be related in some distant fashion, because that is where my folks are from. The same is true of people with my father's name. So there is a feeling of kinship built into our D.N.A. I do believe.

If this IS the case, then it would also be a part of my theory that this is a part of God's larger plan for mankind and that every individual on earth, from the beginning, has been a part of such a family or group that have known each other previously, in Heaven (or whatever you might call the existence beyond the limited life on earth) and we will continue to know and associate with each other after this present life is over. It would explain why we always seem to have a warm feeling when we meet someone who has lived where we used to live or known someone that we have known, as was the case when we met that first couple on the cruise. It would also give meaning to the fact that we met this couple the first thing after I had asked God to lead us to people that He wanted us to meet.

Anyway, I do enjoy saying it! "It's a small world!"

CHAPTER 25: SPECIAL GUESTS

It was during the Christmas season of 1958. The family, which usually lived in the city, was spending the holidays in the country. The snow was falling and the mother asked her 10 year old son, Charley, if he would like to take a drive in the snow. Charley thought that would be a grand idea, so they headed out in the car.

The snow was beautiful, quiet, and clean – not dirty like in the city. As they drove along, the snow began to fall much more heavily. Although the mother was driving very carefully, they slid into a snow bank and the mother could not get traction to back out, even with the son pushing the car. The mother said, "Don't worry, Charlie, I see a house up ahead and I am sure they will let us call for help."

They trudged up to the house and knocked on the door. A lady opened the door and the mother explained their predicament. The lady of the house was happy to have them come in and use the phone. They chatted and had tea while they waited for help to come.

It was a day that young Charlie would never forget, for it was "the day that he and Mum got snowbound!" It was a day that the lady of the house would never forget because it was "the day that Queen Elizabeth and her son, Charles, the heir to the British throne, were unexpected guests in my home!"

In Hebrews 13:2, Paul makes a very surprising statement. "Let brotherly love continue. Be not forgetful to entertain strangers, for thereby some have entertained Angels unawares." Paul was saying that, in helping other people in any way, you are introducing God and Heaven's presence into our daily lives. For those few moments your unexpected guest is God!

In Mathew 25 we see the scene described by Jesus, in which He compliments those who stand before Him in Heaven by saying,

"You saw me sick or in prison or as a stranger and you ministered to my needs and I really appreciate that!" Those who heard were stunned. They could not remember having ever ministered to Jesus. Then Jesus said, "When you did it to other people in need, you were doing it unto Me!" Their unexpected guest was Jesus!

In Mathew 26:26, Jesus is instituting the Lord's Supper as a sacred experience for His followers. He says, "Take, eat, for this is my body." In other words, symbolically this bread represents "Me". The act of my followers eating it together is interaction with "Me". When you read this next to the scripture that I read earlier it is almost as though Jesus is making both activities as equally sacred and important – the Lord's Supper AND random acts of kindness. In both activities, Jesus is present! As the lady unexpectedly entertained the Queen of England, and, as Paul said, we sometimes unexpectedly entertain angels, we sometimes unexpectedly entertain Jesus himself! Perhaps Jesus would even change the word, "sometimes" to "every time" we do an act of kindness we are ministering to Jesus as well!

Several days ago I went to Lowe's Home Improvement store to buy a storm door. It was a bit heavy for one person to handle, but when the check out lady asked if I needed help, the macho in my ego said, "No, I can handle it!" When I got out to my truck I remember thinking, "I should have asked for help!" Just as I was leaning over to lift one end of the door, I heard someone saying, "Sir! Sir!" As I looked around I saw a young man, a customer not a Lowe's employee. He was hurrying up to me, saying, "Let me help you with that!" I had the immediate and distinct feeling that "here is a young man who is consciously trying to put Christ's teaching into his daily life." Although I ended up just saying something like, "I really appreciate your help. It was a bit heavy for one person." I really wanted to say, "You did it! You did exactly what Christ wants us to do! Well done! Well done! And I could tell by your spirit and by a feeling of Christ's presence that it was your intention to carry out Christ's teaching about helping others!" I was even more sure of it when his parting words were, "Have a blessed day!"

Then, last Wednesday, my wife and I went into a discount bread store to get several loaves of our favorite bread and we put them on the counter. It came to about $6.75. We noticed a younger, blond haired lady ahead of us talking quietly to the cashier but thought nothing about it. The other lady left and I said, "What do I owe?" The cashier said, "You don't owe anything, the lady ahead of you paid for your bread". I was stunned. My wife ran after the lady to thank her. My wife came back in and said, "I couldn't catch her!" The cashier said, "She did not mean for you to!" We were blessed that someone was so kind and thoughtful. The amount of money was not important. It was the kindness and generosity of the gesture that meant so much.

So, let me rephrase Christ's words in Mathew 25. "Any time that you help a friend or a stranger put a heavy door on his truck or lift a heavy burden from her heart by offering a listening ear, Christ is there!Every time you say a word of encouragement or take a meal, or use your car, or work in the soup kitchen, or give a smile, Christ is there! Every time your heart reaches out to another heart, even in prayer, Jesus is there as surely as the Queen of England was present in that lady's house." Christ is there, smiling His smile of gratitude and approval.

CHAPTER 26: THE CASE OF THE MISSING WALLET

Last week end we went to Hilton Head, South Carolina, to celebrate our 56th wedding Anniversary. We had a wonderful time.

On Monday morning I spent several hours painting the interior of a rental house and came home about 2:00 o'clock. As usual, I shed my work clothes and took a shower. When I changed clothes I looked for my wallet and it was not where I usually put it when I come in. I was not disturbed because I sometimes lay it down in other places. I looked in those other places – twice – three times. It was not there! Now I was getting disturbed!

After my wife, Finetta, and I had combed the house, we sat down and remembered that I had not had any occasion to use my wallet since Saturday night when we had gone to the Piggly Wiggly grocery store in Hilton Head. We called there but they had not had any wallet reported. It was time to pray. You remember that I told you last week that I usually pray by writing my prayer and the answer that I hear from God in a notebook. It helps me get a more specific answer to my prayers. So I wrote, asking God if He would please tell me where I could find the wallet. He answered, and I am not joking when I tell you what His answer was! He said, "I will not tell you where it is because that would spoil your fun, but I WILL tell you that you WILL find it today!"

We decided that we would go to the rental house because it had to be there. It was a 26 mile round trip and Finetta had to drive because my driver's license was in my wallet. On the way there, we decided to stop on the way back and make two necessary purchases, since the location of each shop was near the rental house. We needed to buy a new refrigerator and also choose carpet for one of the rooms before we could rent the house. We looked in every square inch of the house, several times, but we could not find the wallet. It just had to be somewhere at home!

On the way home we made our purchases. Finetta had to handle the transactions BECAUSE I DID NOT HAVE MY DRIVER'S LICENSE. As Finetta drove I said, "This must be the fun that God didn't want us to miss!" I must admit, I was being sarcastic.

By now we had been searching for about three hours. We ate supper and looked through the house several more times, extending the search to the garden, where I had picked vegetables earlier in the day.

We decided to call our credit card company in case someone had found the wallet. They canceled the current card and promised to send another one. We decided that, even though we did not want to, we had to go back to the rental house. It simply had to be there! Finetta saw me writing in my notebook and said, "Are you asking God for help?"

I said, "Yes."

She said, "What did He say?"

"You won't believe this," I replied, "He said, 'I will not tell you where it is, but you WILL find it tonight and it WILL be exactly where you put it!"

Finetta drove us back to the rental house and, again, we combed every visible inch where it could have fallen or been laid. Each of us took a separate room. Suddenly I heard Finetta shout, "Don, come quick!" I ran into the hall, where she stood with the wallet in her hand. She was standing by the furnace cabinet and I noticed that the furnace cabinet was open! It was then that a whole scenario flashed back into my memory! When I was almost finished with my painting earlier that day, the doorbell had rung. I was not expecting anyone and, since the house is in a somewhat "rough"neighborhood, I thought of the possibility of house invasion. I hurriedly tossed my wallet into the furnace cabinet. "At least they won't get my wallet," I thought! I looked through the peep hole in the door, but it was a bit clouded and I could not tell anything about the visitors. I cautiously opened the door. It turned out to be the prospective renters, wanting to see the house again. By the time they left it was almost time to wrap up my things and go home. I never thought about the wallet again!

Well, as we went home, with ME driving, we were laughing! We really had enjoyed the adventure, even though it was upsetting at the same time. By the time we got home we had had seven hours of FUN!

Now I knew, just as soon as Finetta found the wallet, that I had another potential subject for a devotional. I wasn't sure what the lesson would be. I am still not sure. Would it be that we should not let ourselves get caught up in unnecessary suspicion and fear? Probably not, as, in that neighborhood a home invasion would not be too surprising. I was probably acting quite sensibly.

No, I think the point of the story has to do with God's interaction with us. As I have mentioned before, God "nudges"us in many different ways to bring about benefits to us. It also has to do with the fact that God has a sense of humor. It was almost as if God was smiling when He told me that He didn't want to "spoil our fun". He also wants us to have all kinds of rich blessings. Oh, He could have saved us a lot of time if he had just told us, early on, "Don't you remember, you tossed it into the cabinet when the doorbell rang?" But what would have been the fun in that? Ho hum!

But God allowed us time to build up an exciting amount of suspense and mystery! He motivated me on two different occasions to prayer in which I depended on Him for help. It did help for Him to assure me twice that I would find the wallet and that I would find it that same day. He also allowed us the occasion to make two purchases that we really needed to make anyway. He gave us a good laugh and a good night's sleep. He increased my faith in His ability and willingness to help. After all, we did find it the same day and it was right where I had put it. Just like He said! He also reminded us again that He does not always help us in the way that we want but always in the way that is best. Perhaps best of all, He provided me with another devotional!

CHAPTER 27: THE FLIGHT SIMULATOR

I must give full credit to my cousin, Bob*, who lives in Savannah, for all of my experiences on the computer. I had no computer and no interest in having one until Bob called one night and said, "Don, do you live near Daniel Field?"

I said, "Yes, just down the street."

He said, "Describe where you live in relation to the airport."

I told him that you would "go down Wrightsboro Rd. toward the river" and gave a few more details.

Bob said, "I'm flying over your neighborhood right now! I took off from Daniel Field in my flight simulator and am roughly over your house at the present moment."

Well, he had my attention and it wasn't long before I had a computer AND a flight simulator. Of course the computer has been a wonderful help to my writing since the first day that I got it.

But, let me tell you more about my flight simulator. I have a choice of about twenty different airplanes that I can choose from, beginning with the Wright Brothers' first airplane and going all the way to the Boeing 747 and every size airplane in between. Flying the simulator is like sitting in the cockpit of the real thing. I can take off from any of thousands of airports all over the world and fly over simulations of almost any sight in the world. I have landed on the water in front of the Taj Mahal Palace, flown over Niagara Falls, under the Brooklyn Bridge, landed on the Great Wall of China, on the lawn in front of the Washington Monument and in the desert in front of the Great Pyramids of Egypt. It is a wonderful experience to see all of these things from the safety of one's own den.

You can be as technical as you wish. You can choose to learn every switch and function in every airplane and make it so that you have to do everything in the proper sequence in order to fly – just as if you were flying the real airplane. Or, on the other hand, you can choose to be able to switch "On" and take off immediately, with very little knowledge of flying. So, you can enjoy flying as a trained expert or you can just enjoy the thrill of "flying through the air" as an amateur, learning as you go. It is entirely up to you how deeply you want to get involved.

I truly believe that that is also a good description of the Christian experience. God does not coerce us all to be equally involved in our Christian experience. Some feel lead to go into Christian work full time. Most of us are happy to do what we can in our spare time. In other words, in terms of flying, we are glad to learn how to take off and land. You have heard me say before that each of us comes to earth with certain things to learn and certain things that we have come to accomplish. I do not believe that we all came to earth with the intention of becoming equally immersed in the work of the church nor did we all come here with the plan of becoming Bible scholars. So, if you did not become a full time minister that is fine with God. Perhaps it was His intention for you to become a good business man or a Christian housewife and mother.

When I was a boy of 9, it was my ambition to become a Marine pilot and fly a Corsair fighter plane. When I grew up I never did that. But I really enjoy flying my Corsair fighter on the simulator! That is enough. Perhaps there was a time in your early life when you thought that maybe God wanted you to do this or that great thing in His kingdom. It is even possible that you think perhaps you let Him down by not doing more. My word to you is this. God very likely had His hand in every turn that your life has made. So be grateful for life and for where your life has led you thus far. As well as you can, be open to wherever God will lead you during the rest of your life. Enjoy flying your Christian life at whatever level of expertise the Lord has given you so far. Trust Him to take you deeper if He wishes.

In none of what I am saying do I mean to trivialize your Christian experience in any way. What I am trying to say is that, just as I can thoroughly enjoy flying at the level that I have reached, without feeling bad that I never became a Marine pilot, I believe that God wants each of us to enjoy our Christian walk and worship at whatever level we have attained thus far, with the full awareness that He has not finished with us yet! He has a whole eternity to mold us and make us! He will let you know when and if He wants you to do more!

*Name has been changed for the sake of privacy.

CHAPTER 28: THE SACREDNESS OF OUR BODIES

This devotional is going to fit into that category of themes in which you will possibly say, "Now, preacher, you've quit preaching and gone to meddling!" If so, I am as sorry as you are, for it hits me every bit as hard as it hits you. But, when I ask the Lord for a subject and He gives it to me, I do feel some obligation to use it unless I have a good reason not to. This time I could not come up with a good reason not to! So, I will suffer with you.

There is a line which should be drawn between what is good for someone's body and what is not. That line should be diligently respected, studied, and attended to by all who seek to please God. Remember that Paul said, in 1 Cor. 6:19, that our body is the temple of the Holy Spirit. If that is the case, then keeping our body healthy is not as much an optional consideration as we have come to think of it. Yes, we respect our church sanctuary and we would never even consider for a moment throwing a bag of garbage in the aisle of the church or emptying our automobile's ashtray onto the altar of our church. So tell me why the church building where you worship should be more sacred than the temple that houses the Holy Spirit of God? I know, you just never thought of it like that before. Neither had I until the Lord gave me this devotional. So please do not shoot the messenger!

Now, this line that I spoke of, that divides what is good for our body from what is not, this line changes based on the knowledge that we have. The knowledge that they had in Bible times was quite different from what it would be now. There is so much that we know today about how to stay healthy that Paul and Peter did not know. So we are responsible for that extra knowledge! I know. It doesn't seem fair but I believe that is the way things are. It is even easier to see if we look at what our parents and grand parents knew and compare it to what we know today. Take smoking, for instance. Millions of our service men smoked during World War II. Most of our parents smoked. They might have been told that it was "a nasty habit" but they did not have any idea what it was doing to their lungs and lips and mouths. But you and I know what smoking can do and therefore we are held to a higher standard where smoking is concerned. To our credit, most of us who smoked in our younger years have had the wisdom, strength, and will to quit in our later years.

Now that brings us to where the battle field is today. Healthy eating habits and weight control is an area that it is so easy to joke about and take lightly. Today's news is full of stories of school officials and other people who work with children trying to weed out snacks, drinks, and fast foods that are making our children obese at an early age. Many of us adults, including myself, are not very good role models for our children and grandchildren. We tend to take the view of "Do what we say, not what we do." But they tend to follow what they have seen in our behavior regardless. If we continue to consider overeating and poor food choice as a laughing matter, our children will begin to die at an earlier and earlier age. Their bodies are the temples of God! Do we believe that?

We can make the same case for exercise. Most of us are, perhaps, somewhat past jogging. But we can still walk. We might not be able to lift heavy weights, but our arms, shoulders, and chest muscles need whatever we are capable of lifting or moving routinely to keep them healthy. That line of knowledge is there now and we can not claim that we just did not know! We are responsible to God for what we know about keeping our body healthy.

I am simply saying that, in the sight of God, it is not enough to have a strict discipline about overuse of alcohol, unchristian sexual activity, and other "no-no's" that we have been brought up with and then blink at, or even laugh at, the abuse of our body at a fast food restaurant or at our kitchen table.

So, let us each ask God to give us a more serious and willing attitude where the health of our body is concerned. Let us take responsibility for what we know already and what we will learn over the coming years about keeping the temple of God, our body, as healthy and pure as we are capable of doing. Amen.

CHAPTER 29: THE THANKSGIVING PLANT

(I am holding a beautiful Christmas Cactus plant as I give this devotional).

You will probably recognize this plant as a Christmas Cactus, but I call it our Thanksgiving Plant! You see, it belonged to my wife's mother. She died over 35 years ago and we know that she had it several years, so we feel that a conservative estimate is that it is at least 40 years old! After the mother's death it was passed to my wife's brother, who later passed it to us. We have had it for about 19 years.

It had not been in good health for several years and we were concerned about it. It was down to a few straggly leaves with no blooms. My wife asked our friend and neighbor, a Master gardener, about it. She said, "Let me take it home and do a few things to it." Not only did she bring it back big, healthy, and producing blooms, but she has another plant just like it that came from the original.

This devotional was originally presented during the Thanksgiving season and several elements of this story form my own personal reasons for giving thanks. I would like to share these with you.

My wife's mother and her brother represent our source from the past. Of course, God is our ultimate source, but those who have lived before us are our immediate source of help as we mature. Just as we received this plant and its beauty from them, in that same way we received much that we are thankful for from those who lived before us – our education, our traditions, our values, our nation, our very lives came from them.

The plant itself, passed on to us, represents all that came to us as gifts – our spouse, our children, our work, friends, church, and so much more!

The change between the scrawny thing that it was and the beautiful, healthy plant that it is now represents the power of renewal. Our whole body is renewing itself all the time. But beyond that, God can take us when we are sick, worried, or discouraged and renew us like a Master Gardener! We, as friends, can have a part in that renewal, working to help each other as our friend worked to renew our plant.

The extended life of the plant reminds me that you and I, those of us over 70 years of age, have already been blessed with extended life. Most of us have already enjoyed life beyond the average life span. All that comes to us now is like "icing on the cake".

What happened when our plant was renewed gives me a hint as to what will happen to us. Our bodies are all in some stage of decline. In a sense we are somewhat like the plant was before our friend took it. But, in God's time, we will become fresh and new – no more pain, sorrow, tears, medicines, or losses. We will be brand new when we go to be with God.

CHAPTER 30: THEY FILLED IN

There were several times in my childhood when I was an "only child", living with a single parent – my mother. This fact certainly could have caused me untold problems if it were not for the fact that many people were able to "fill in the gap" that was left by the absence of a father figure in my life. It is those "gap fillers"that I would like to honor in this little reflection. The purpose of this exercise is that you might recognize and appreciate the "gap fillers"in your own life and that you might see that you have also served such a purpose in the lives of others and that you still have the potential to do so until the moment that you pass from this earth.

In my own life, I remember my first grade teacher. It was on a day when someone took my lunch. Lunch time came and I was going to be hungry. My teacher lived about a block from the school. Times were different then and no teacher could take such a chance now, but she gave me the key to her house, told me where the crackers, peanut butter, and milk were located, and told me to eat as much as I wanted. That teacher taught me about trust and compassion and gave me an experience of independence.

In my church life there were so many who filled the gap, but my Royal Ambassador Leader and her husband (Royal Ambassadors was a boys group, similar to Boy Scouts, in my church) showed great respect and allowed me to take on jobs and challenges that built my confidence and experience to the degree that, when I was in the tenth grade I became a Royal Ambassador leader myself. The Florida State Ambassador Leader even had me come one summer and serve as a camp counselor. Later I participated in his wedding. Such was the influence of one couple on a nine year old boy!

When I was 11 and in the fifth grade, Mr. Ihler, my principal, gave me the job of setting up the 16 mm. Film projector to show the weekly school movie. He also had me ride my bicycle up town to the school supply store when he ran out of supplies. Again, my confidence and work ethic were being nurtured.

The same principal, Mr. Ihler, was the choir director at my church. He had me singing in the church adult church choir when I was just 12 years old.

Also, when I was in the fifth grade, Mrs. Moore, who was a first grade teacher but also in charge of the school Safety Patrol, allowed me to be one of her Safety Patrol "boys". My duty was to come to school 30 minutes early and stay 30 minutes after school to help the policeman stop traffic and usher boys and girls across a very busy Montgomery Street in west Savannah – at 38th Street Elementary School. I got to wear a white web cross belt and badge and took my responsibility very seriously. In fact, as I recall, the policeman spent much of his time in a nearby store drinking coffee, while I directed traffic. (That was then. I know they would not do that today!)

All of these people, and many more, gave me the sort of help that you would ordinarily expect from a father. But, because they were there, my life did not suffer.

Much of the "gap filling"was also done by my extended family. I alternated between living with my grand parents and my aunt and uncle during the years that I was in the third through the sixth grades. When I was with my grand parents I learned to do and think independently. I had chores, like bringing in the coal for the pot bellied stove. I was allowed to go on the bus up town to the movies and the wrestling matches, dancing classes and even to lectures at Armstrong Junior College! That might seem strange for a fifth grader but, at the time it seemed quite natural.

During this time I also lived part time with my aunt and uncle, who had a daughter younger than me, a son about my age, and a son a little older. The son that was my age became like a brother and we did many things and learned many things together. All of this was between 9 and 12 years of age.

Now, I have told you about these "gap fillers", partly to show how God provides what is needed in our lives and partly to encourage each of us to be aware of our own opportunities to be such gap fillers to others in our own lives. At times, I know that some of you have helped relatives by allowing them to stay in your home for a while. At other times you might have just given a word of encouragement. Whatever it has been in the past or might be in the future – to a child or to an adult - please remember that you have been God's helper in filling in the otherwise empty parts of another person's life.

You might want to look around for any present opportunities for being such a gap filler. There are still many places for people our age to serve. There are places in Sunday School, the mid week children's activities, and the extended session during the worship service. Remember, there are still organizations such as Boy Scouts, Girl Scouts, hospice and many others that can still use our time and energy during the course of a week.

In doing all of this, in the past and present, you will have earned the admonition that Mordecai gave to Esther (Esther 4:14) - "Who knows but that you have been sent here (by God) for such a time as this?"

CHAPTER 31: THINGS THAT LAST

I do not mean to get too philosophical, but I would like to talk about God for a minute and not in church terms but in even more basic terms than that. If you have ever had even a moment's doubt that maybe there isn't really a God after all - if you have ever had that thought for even a minute, as scary as it seems to talk about it, then this is for you. It really is for all of us. My question for you is, "what are the things that will last forever?"

When I lived in Jacksonville, Florida, in 1955, I was still dating. The place to go on a date was the drive in theater! I have an old Jacksonville telephone book and I counted the number of drive in theaters we had in 1955. Would you believe, in a town of maybe 250,000 at that time, we had 12 drive in theaters? I would guess that there are probably none now. I do not know if television pushed them out or if it was just an idea that came and went. But it did not last.

When my oldest son was in Junior High school in the mid 70's, a wonderful new fad came into existence – the Citizen's Band radio. For young people and adults alike, C.B was like a kid getting his first secret code ring from Captain America. We just could not get enough. My "handle" was "Yellow Bug"and my son was "wolf man". Almost everyone had a C.B in their home or car or both. Someone would be talking on the C.B every night until at least midnight. But now you would be hard pressed to find a vehicle with a C.B antenna if you looked in every parking lot in town. A very hot idea that came and went. It did not last.

When my wife and I first came to Augusta, Ga in 1970, another very hot idea was trading stamps. There were green stamps and there were yellow stamps. Almost every store had to give you some sort of stamps or you just would not trade there – grocery stores, gas stations, hardware stores – all gave trading stamps! There were catalogs that showed you how many stamps you needed in order to get a television set or a frying pan. But at some point even green and yellow stamps went out of style. They did not last either.

It is very hard to tell what new thing will last and what will run its course and leave us. I am sure that some people thought that television would be a fad, but it has stayed and simply evolved over the years. Others might still think that computers will never last but I would not hold my breath about that one.

But what is it that will never fade? What is it that has been with mankind for as far back as we can dig and find remnants?

The simple Christian answer is God, of course. But I would like to go beyond the answer that you would expect from a minister. To me there are several basics that go beyond some other arguments for the existence of God. I believe that man has been found to have at least three needs for as far back as we have any records, even from pictures on cave walls. First, man needs food and water or he will die physically. Therefore food and water is a basic need. If man was created with such a need, it follows that there will be something that will meet that need. That need and its fulfillment will never pass away as long as man lives on earth.

Secondly, as far back as we go in records, we find that man has shown a need for social interaction with other people. If he does not have this interaction he will die mentally and/or emotionally. There have been exceptions to this but by and large, man depends heavily on social interaction for his health. So, again, it follows that if mankind exhibits a basic need for fellowship, there will be something in the created order to satisfy this need. That something is man's peer group. Neither the need nor what is provided to supply that need will ever pass away.

Lastly, the third basic need that has always showed up when we study the history of mankind is his consistent reflection of a belief in the supernatural and in life beyond his earthly existence. This shows up especially in his burial rituals and practices. Much that we have found in ancient man points to a need to believe in a hereafter and in a supreme being beyond ourselves. So, following the same logic that we have used before, if a basic need of man seems to be a belief in God, then it follows that there will be something in the created order to meet that need. That which meets that need is God Himself.

So, although drive in theaters, green stamps, C.B radios, and many other things may come and go in our world, three things will always remain as long as there is man – the need for food and water for the body and also the food and water to meet that need, the need for socialization with our fellow man and the means to meet that need, and the need for spiritual food for the soul and God to meet that need.

These three will last for as long as mankind lives on earth.

With that said, we must realize that mankind will always put his own particular labels and twists on the food and water, on the types of socialization, and on their concept of God. Thus the way that each religious group sees and understands God will be different. But I think that the fact that mankind needs all three of these basics is one of the best arguments for the existence of God that we can have. The fact that men differ in how they see God is not the point here. What I am saying is, if men feel this basic need to believe in God, then I think that there must be a God that is drawing out this need to believe. It is this God that Abraham worshiped. It is the same God that I have worshiped from my childhood and always will, even though He might not look and sound exactly the same to me and to Abraham. He is the same God, yesterday, today, and forever. He will last forever and our relationship with Him will last forever.

CHAPTER 32: THREE MODELS FOR LIFE

Christ often taught with the aid of similes – saying that one thing is like another. Usually this took the form of comparing a less understood item with one that is more common. For instance, He said that the kingdom of God is like a mustard seed, or like leaven in a loaf of bread, or like a treasure that a man found.

When I try to express my philosophy of life, I have found that there are three similes or models that bring out my beliefs most clearly. Life is like a school, a game, and a drama.

First of all, I like to compare life to a school. I believe that we come to earth with several goals. We come to learn certain lessons. We also come to accomplish definite objectives. Lastly, we come to help others – family, friends and strangers - in fulfilling all of their goals.

We learn our lessons from the events in our lives. Each one of us has a different curriculum, designed just for us. God designs the curriculum with our welfare in mind. Whatever happens to me, I consider to be part of the curriculum and I look for the lesson in that event.

Some of our goals are personal and involve only ourselves. Others involve other people. We will leave the earth only when all of our learning and helping goals are fulfilled, not before. When we have learned the prescribed curriculum and fulfilled all of our goals, we graduate to a higher grade. That is really all that "death" is – a graduation.

Life is also like a game. A game is always a temporary arrangement. We always assume that a game has a beginning and an ending and then all of the temporary provisions of the game cease to be. Then we go home. We would not have it any other way. As I said, a game is temporary. It is different from real life. I might enjoy football, even play the game. But football is not real life. In that same sense, the life that we are now living on earth is enjoyable, but it also is temporary. Our real, real life is what we go back to when this "game of life" is over. Our real life is in God, with God – that which we typically call Heaven. God has allowed us to participate, temporarily, in the game of life for the same reasons that we play a game like Monopoly - for our enjoyment, growth, and fellowship with others.

We should never take the game too seriously. In a game of Monopoly, somebody owns Boardwalk, someone always owns more hotels than other folk, and someone goes directly to jail. But when the game is over, we say goodbye and go home. It really doesn't matter who owned Boardwalk! In life we have the ability to stop, back up, and say, "This is just a game. None of this is of great importance within itself – only the results. The game will end and it really doesn't matter what I owned but what I learned, how I enjoyed it, how I played the game, and how I helped others!" Most of our problems in life come from our forgetting some of the above.

Lastly, life is like a drama. My life has a story line. So does yours. My story effects the story of everyone else in my drama - from my wife and children all the way to the girl who checks me out at Kroger grocery.

I personally believe that the cast of characters in each person's drama is arranged in Heaven by the same loving God who arranged our curriculum in life as a school. I would not be surprised if we each also had a part in making those arrangements before we were even born.

I believe that our characters and dialogues all fit together and what we say and do is somewhat dependent on each others' words and actions.

Have you ever been to a high school play when a character's next line is, "I wonder who that is at the door?" But someone forgets to knock on the door. So the character can not say what he was supposed to say and the whole play is thrown off. I believe that what we say and do to each other is very important because we never know when that might be like the knock on the door that keeps his life drama going. Or, it might need to be said to keep our own drama moving along.

When our part in the drama is over, we make our exit. We make our exit at just the right time – not too soon and not too late. We will have said and done all that we were meant to say and do.

When we do make our exit we hope, of course, that those who are still in the play will think that we played our part well. But we can be sure that, backstage, God and those who have already exited the drama will be giving us a standing ovation. God will be saying, "Well done! Bravo! Well done!"

CHAPTER 33: CONVERSATIONAL PRAYER

If you look in the Bible you will probably find every form of prayer that we use today: Public prayer, recited ritual prayer (the way we often use the Lord's Prayer), prayer on behalf of others, prayer for forgiveness and reconciliation, and many other forms of prayer. But there is one form of prayer that we seldom practice – conversation with God. Conversation implies that you speak and God speaks back. Then you respond to God and He responds back. It is the kind of conversation that Moses had with God about leading His people out of Egypt. Do you remember that? God said something like, "Moses, I want you to go to Pharaoh and tell him to let my people go!"

"Who? Me, God? I can't do that!"

"Sure you can, Moses!" etc.

That was prayer, but it certainly was not one sided, as many of our prayers are today. It was a two sided conversation with God.

But, perhaps you are thinking, "That kind of conversational prayer only happens in the Bible!" But I am here to tell you that it CAN happen today if you EXPECT it to happen!

How do you usually pray? Chances are that your praying is something like this. You might ask God to DO something, which might be something that you want to have happen - "Please help me to know what to do about...." or "Please let my son, John, find a job!" Then God's answer might be that I would have a feeling about what I should do or John would either get the job or not. But then, after you "get the feeling" you might doubt whether you got the RIGHT feeling or not.

That is exactly the way I prayed for much of my life. I did not expect an immediate answer from God as I would expect from you if I asked you a question. But then, one day, I read a book about prayer. In the book there was an unusual statement, something like this: "If you will write out your prayer in the form of a conversation and actually EXPECT an answer from God, and then write out the answer that you 'hear in your heart', then you can actually get a much more immediate and specific answer from God."

That was a very exciting statement for me! After all, when I began to feel the call of God to the ministry, I was in the tenth grade of high school. I was not sure if God was really calling me or if I just wanted to be a minister. I prayed sincerely and regularly for God's answer all through high school and into college, without getting the definite answer that I longed to hear. Now, if I have an occasion in which I need an answer like that, my prayer would be more like, "God, is this something that you want me to do?" Then, I would expect to get an immediate answer like, "Yes, Donald, I would like very much to see you do that" or "No, Donald, I would much rather that you do such and such...". In some cases certain events must take place before His answer can be clear. But in most situations, when we need information or direction, or assurance, prayer can bring much more immediate and specific help than we typically expect. I will give you several examples:

When I had my knee replacement several years ago, I had a discomfort behind my knee several days after I got home. The doctor thought that I might have a blood clot forming and said that I might have to begin taking a blood thinner. He made an appointment for a sonogram. I was very worried and I did not want to take a blood thinner. I prayed and asked God if I had a blood clot. I received an immediate answer in which God said, "Donald, you do NOT have a blood clot and you will NOT have to take a blood thinner!" The sonogram proved Him right on both counts!

On another occasion I went to Miami to help my son move into a new apartment. We were trying to mount a very old, ornate mirror over his bathroom sink. It had a wire across the top, so that it could be hung on a nail. But it weighed almost 50 pounds and I was afraid to mount that much weight with a wire and a nail. If it fell, it could easily hurt or kill someone. We took a break and I asked God for help. I wrote the request because it is easier to get a clear response if I write it down. Here is the immediate answer that I received. "Donald. On each corner of the wooden mirror frame is a brass decoration that will slip off. Take all four of the brass ornaments off and drill a hole in each corner. Hold the mirror in place and drive a two inch screw through one corner hole and into the wall. Then drill another screw through each of the other corners and into the wall while keeping the mirror lined up properly. It will then be very safe and secure. Then replace all of the brass decorations." It worked perfectly, of course!

A third example also happened in Miami, and is an example of how you can get a very specific answer from God even when you can not write the prayer, if necessary. I was at my son's apartment and he was in the hospital after an operation. It was late at night and I had a pain in my chest. I thought I might be having a heart attack. It was about 1:00 o'clock in the morning. I went to one hospital emergency room and it looked so dark and gloomy that I decided to go to another hospital that I knew was a better hospital. As I was hurrying to the other hospital I recognized the voice of God saying, "Donald, please, please turn around and go back to that convenience store you just passed and get some antacid tablets. That is ALL you need." I heard this sentence clearly enough that I had confidence that it was God. I did as I was told and went back to the apartment for a good night's sleep.

It is my belief that many of the very specific answers to prayer that we read about in the Bible, were specific because the person praying expected specific answers and was used to getting very clear and specific answers to prayer. You might want to try this approach to prayer when you have time this afternoon. Just keep in mind two things. First, there is nothing magical about writing down the prayer but it just seems to help us hear the answer and keep it clear in our mind as we write it down. Secondly, we tend to hear God's answer clearly and specifically if we EXPECT to hear it that way. If we are in the habit of NOT really expecting a clear answer to our prayers, then that is exactly what we will get!

Try to pray using the following suggestions:

Think of a question that you would like to ask God.

Write down your prayer. An example might be, "Dear Father, is there anything that you would like for me to do? Thank You." (I usually include 'Thank you' in my prayer because the attitude of thankfulness seems to help when we pray.)

Then write down anything that you seem to hear deep in your heart. It might take a bit of practice before this answer comes freely, but the main thing at first is to write down whatever comes. No one is going to see this but you and God anyway. With practice you will hear the answer quickly, easily, and freely. After a while you will easily be able to distinguish between God's words and all of the jumble of thoughts that you might sometimes "hear"in your head. Also, after some practice with written prayers, you will find that, in a pinch, you can get the same immediate and specific answer without writing down your prayer.

May God bless you with a fresh, new and exciting relationship to God in your prayer life!

PRAYER: "Dear Father, please help us all to expect and experience an ever increasing closeness to You in our prayer life. We ask in Christ's name. Amen."

CHAPTER 34: TWO CONVERSATIONS

(This devotional was also included in my first devotional book, "My Best To You Each Morning", but I am including it here because it is probably my favorite and also because it has been so well received.)

One evening, as I was searching for a theme for this devotional, I noticed that "Fiddler on the Roof" was on the evening movie list. It is one of my favorite movies and I felt that, perhaps, God would use it to give me a subject. He did!

The movie is about Tevye, the village milk man, and his wife and daughters. The setting is Tsarist Russia in 1905. Tevye and his wife, Golde, were married in the traditional Jewish way, chosen for each other by a "match maker", with no thought of love or personal choice on the part of either.

Their lives were complicated because their three older daughters, within a short time, had made choices of husbands that defied their beloved tradition. The first daughter, after being promised to the local, well- to- do butcher, persuaded Tevye to give his permission for her to marry a poor tailor instead. Tevye did this, in spite of tradition, because he saw the "love in her eyes" for the tailor.

This new experience of seeing love and marriage together caused Tevye to rethink his own marriage, and as he approached Golde a very beautiful musical conversation ensued.

Tevye: "Do you love me?"

Golde: "Do I what!?"

Tevye: "Do you love me?"

Golde: "Do I love you? For 25 years I've washed your clothes, cooked your meals, cleaned your house,given you children, milked you cow. After 25 years, why talk about love right now?"

Tevye: The first time I met you was on our wedding day. I was scared."

Golde: "I was shy."

Tevye: "I was nervous."

Golde: "So was I"

Tevye: "But my father and my mother said we'd learn to love each other, and now I am asking. Golde, do you love me?"

Golde: "I'm your wife!"

Tevye: "I know, but do you love me?"

Golde: "Do I love him? For 25 years I've lived with him, fought with him, starved with him. 25 years my bed is his, If that's not love, what is?"

Tevye: "Then you do love me."

Golde: "I suppose I do.

Tevye: "And I suppose I love you too."

Both: "It doesn't change a thing. But even so, after 25 years it's nice to know."

Now, as I heard this tender interchange, it dawned on me that this could be a conversation between God and myself. Let me present it to you just as I heard it.

God: "Donald, do you love me?"

Myself: "Do I what?"

God: "Do you love me?"

Myself: "Do I love you? I must be imagining this!"

God: "No, Donald. This is God and I am asking

you a question. Do you love me?"

Myself: "Do I love You? For 69 years I've gone to church, Sunday School and Training Union. You remember Training Union, God?

God: "Yes, Donald. Was that 69 years ago? Yes, it was. I remember when we first met – really met. You were ten years old and you were at a funeral. It was the first time you realized that people really do die. For the first time you realized that some day you would be in a casket just like that."

Myself: "Yes, God. I was scared. Soon after that I became a Christian. The pastor said that I would learn to love you."

God: "So, do you love me?"

Myself: "For Heaven's sake, God. I'm a Christian!

God: "I know. But, do you love me?"

Myself: "Do I love Him? For 69 years I've prayed to Him, told other people all about Him, even built my career on Him, if that's not love what is?

God: "So, you DO love me?"

Myself: "God, if I know my heart, I love You more than anything else in the whole wide world!"

God: "And I love you too, Donald. More than anything else in the whole wide world! It doesn't change a thing but even so, after 69 years, it's nice to know."

God is still asking that question of each of us, and we each must answer as we see fit.

Let us pray. "Dear Father. We DO love you. Please help us to love you more. We ask in Christ's name. Amen"

CHAPTER 35: UNEXPECTED BLESSINGS.

This book, "My Best To You At Eventide", has a picture of a
sunset on the front cover. My other devotional book, "My Best To
You Each Morning", has a picture of a sunrise. That seems only
fair. But the sunrise picture came from the printer's image library.
This sunset picture came from my own camera. It is my favorite
nature picture of all time. It is beautiful. But what makes it my
favorite is that I received an unexpected blessing when I took it.
My wife and I had taken our very first "bus tour", two years ago,
into Vermont, to "see the turning of the leaves". We had a
wonderful time and on one particular evening our group had eaten
at a restaurant overlooking beautiful Lake Champlain. After dinner
we went out onto the deck, with our camera, of course, and joined
the others who were watching a beautiful sunset.

I decided that there was no way to know when the most perfect
color would arrive, so I took a picture about every two minutes as
the sun dropped lower and lower. I was focusing just on the color,
not on the total picture. At the end I knew that the color had gotten
progressively more beautiful. But it was not until we got to our
room that night and reviewed the pictures (on our very first digital
camera) that I realized that the most beautiful picture of all had an
added bonus that was missing in all of the others. During the
interval before I took that last picture, a sailboat had drifted right
into the center of the sun's reflection on the water, making a picture
that could not have been chorcographed any better. I did not even
know that I had captured that scene! I felt that God had something
to do with that.

As I look at my life, there are so many times and ways that God
has added "bonuses" to His blessings. I would like to mention just
a few as illustrations in order to "get you thinking" about how He
has done the same thing in your own life.

Several years ago, my wife and I were living on the south side of
town near the institution where I had served as chaplain. As we got

older, we realized that we needed to live closer to our son and to the doctors and hospitals in case our age brought with it some physical ailments. We began to think in terms of a move. We asked a friend at church how she had found her home, which happened to be in the general area where we wanted to go. She said, "there is a house right across the street from us that is for sale! Please look at it!" We did look at it and we made an offer within a week. We bought it primarily because of its location. But after we moved in we realized that God had really been "looking after us". Every window had been replaced with double pane thermal windows. The half basement was an added blessing that we had not even considered. The neighborhood is a community minded, street lighted neighborhood where you can walk safely after dark and where seasonal invitations are extended for meals and parties, teas and coffees. So much that we had not expected! The house that we moved from sold within a week to our next door neighbor! Bonuses from God!

The same thing happened several years ago when we traded automobiles. We traded to a new brand at the recommendation of our son, who had one of their cars and was very pleased with everything about it. We traded based on the price and the color. But after trading, we had a built in bonus that we did not even know existed. It was what we now know as XM radio. The car came with the receiver built in and a year of free service. We absolutely would not have a car without XM radio if we had any choice at all. It is wonderful! We hear 1940's music and the old early radio shows, like Jack Benny, Bob Hope, and Fibber McGee and Molly - so much of the nostalgia that my wife and I grew up with.

When I was a little boy my mother would sometimes bring me some cracker jack. It had a wonderful sweet snack inside the box but it also came with a little prize inside. I feel that God has done that sort of thing for me all of my life. He has given me many blessings, but He has also included little bonus prizes along with the main gift. I really never know what to expect when He gets ready to bless me.

Prayer: "Dear Father. Thank you for the challenges of life that cause me to grow. Thank you for the disappointments that make me lean on You. And thank You for the unexpected blessings that you hide here and there that give me joy. In Christ's name. Amen"

CHAPTER 36: MY FIRST WHITE ACRE PEAS

My wife and I married in 1956. Shortly after our marriage I was called to my first church as a Baptist minister. It was a small country church in Fulton, Kentucky. I was a city boy but my wife grew up in the country and in a small country church. She knew how country folks thought and helped me to avoid many mistakes that my ignorance of country ways might have precipitated. She also gave me a great deal of help in communicating with my church members and also in doing things that would allow me to grow closer to them.

One of those fundamental things happened to be to plant a garden. I had never done anything like that before and hardly knew which end of a hoe went into the dirt. But I really wanted to learn and found my church flock very eager to help me. So even from my first garden I had a good harvest and was absolutely thrilled. As a result I have had at least a passable garden all but two years since that first one. That makes about fifty gardens in all.

Well, I stuck to the regular vegetables - green beans, tomatoes, bell peppers, egg plant, yellow and zucchini squash and okra. I had a few early gardens with lettuce, radishes, and swiss chard, but mostly stayed with the later fare. I did try corn one year but right at harvest time, when I was so proud of myself, I found the ears full of worms. I dearly hate any kind of worms but fishing worms. Which brings me to the heart of this story.

At some time during those fifty gardens, my wife bought some white acre peas from the grocery store. My, they were good! We both agreed that I should add these heavenly peas to my next garden. So I did. I paid special attention to those little darlings and kept the bugs off and such, gave them just enough water and fertilizer, etc. Oh, they turned out nice and big and healthy looking. We were so excited when we picked our first mess of those little beauties. I helped her shell them too. She put on a big pot of them for supper.

Well, we sat down and I took a big ladle full on my plate with rice and meat and corn bread. This was going to be pretty close to

Heaven tonight! After I took a few bites I noticed some little worms no bigger than an eighth of an inch each and each one of them was curved like a half moon. I had never seen anything like it. I said, "Honey, look at this! These little old worms. How did we miss them? We were careful in shelling and washing and we didn't see them then!" Well, there was nothing to do but throw that whole pot full in the garbage cause they were all through that whole pot. It sure ruined our supper that night.

When another mess was ready we picked and shelled and washed and looked ever so carefully and we were quite sure this time that there were none of those little critters in this batch! But you guessed it. When they were all cooked and ready and smelling wonderful, we looked in the pot and they were there again. In the garbage they went again. My wife said, "Why don't you ask the men at the deacons' meeting tonight what they do to get rid of those worms".

"Oh, that's a good idea," I agreed.

That night, as the men were making small talk before the meeting, I explained what had happened to us, including the throwing out of the two pots of the peas. They all shook their heads in bewilderment. None of them had had any problems with worms in their white acre peas. Then one of the men looked like a light went on in his head. "Now, were these worms really small, like maybe an eighth of an inch? Were they kind of curved like a half moon?"

"That's them exactly", I said.

The light went on in all of the men's heads at once and they all looked like they couldn't decide whether to laugh or cry. Finally one the men said, "Preacher, I don't know exactly how to tell you this but you poured out two big pots of good peas, because all those little "worms" were nothing but the the little bitty piece of the pea that always comes off when they are cooked?" Well, you can imagine that I was stunned speechless. Then I couldn't quite decide whether to laugh or cry. But finally I did laugh. In fact we all laughed a whole lot after that. You know, I always felt a little closer to the men in that church after that. But they did have fun for a long time, asking the preacher how his white acre peas were coming along!

One of the things that I learned from our White Acre Pea experience is not to judge too quickly by appearance. The other night I came across a video on the computer of one of those talent shows - the British version of America's Got Talent. A duet came on the stage – a pretty girl and a very overweight person that, at first, I was not sure about the gender. It turned out to be a very obese young man with shoulder length hair. As the camera panned around the audience and the judges you could see on their faces such thoughts as, "Well, this is a waste of time!" and "What are they doing in a talent show?" The girl was 16 and the boy, 17. The music started and the whole audience said a non verbal "Ho Hum!" But then this beautiful, booming operatic voice came out of this young man and the whole audience got to their feet in disbelief. How easy it is to make White Acre Peas out of people! How often do we "write off" people that we see in the grocery store because of a tattoo or clothes that we do not approve of or some other superficial thing that does not accurately tell us who that person really is. May God give us the grace and the insight not to judge at all. But, if we must judge, and sometimes I suppose we must, let us do it with thoroughness and depth. Not with the casual and uninformed hastiness that we used in our disposal of our White Acre Peas!

CHAPTER 37: A LITTLE GIRL'S PRAYER.   Isaiah 65: 24.
"Before they call, I will answer."

A friend of mine, who lives in Florida, has a daughter. When the
daughter was 5 years old, she was kneeling at her bedside for her
nightly prayer. She ended her prayer saying, "And please, God,
take away this awful cold. Amen" As she got into bed, she sneezed.
"Oh, my goodness!"she said, "I've got another cold!" Such is the
faith of some children in the power of prayer.

I would like to share a story, taken from a personal testimony of
Dr. Helen Roseveare, a British missionary to Zaire, Africa.*

She said that she and her helpers had tried hard to keep a young
mother alive when she had given birth to a premature infant. But
their best efforts failed and the young mother died, leaving the
infant and a 2 year old daughter.

The clinic did not have an incubator or even the electricity to run
one. Nor did they have any special feeding equipment for a
premature infant. All they had was a special box in which to place
the baby and some cotton material to wrap it in. Although they
lived on the equator, the nights could be chilly and windy.

One to the doctor's helpers went to stoke up the fire and fill the hot
water bottle. She came back shortly in great distress. As she was
filling the hot water bottle, it burst. The African climate is hard on
rubber goods. There was no back up for the bottle and no store
anywhere nearby that would have such an item. They slept close to
the infant all night to keep it warm.

The next day at noon, Dr. Roseveare went over to the orphanage,
as was her practice, to have prayer with the children. Among the
things that she suggested for them to remember in prayer was the
situation with the baby and the 2 year old daughter. One of the girls
– 10 year old Ruth – said, "And, God, please send us a hot water
bottle for the baby. It has to come this afternoon. It won't do for it
to come tomorrow or the baby might die!. And also, please send a
dolly for the little girl so that she will know that you love her."

The doctor cringed when she heard Ruth's audacious prayer. She knew that God can do anything, but that the only way that it was likely to happen was by someone sending her a parcel from her homeland. But she had been on the mission field for almost 4 years and had never received a single parcel from anyone. Anyway, if someone were to send a parcel, it would not likely have a hot water bottle, for this was, after all, equatorial Africa.

Half way through the afternoon, as she was teaching at the nurses' training school, someone came and said that there was a car stopped at her front door. By the time she got there, the car was gone. But there was a large box at the door. She was amazed but thrilled. She could not possibly open the box without the children being present, so she sent for them to come.

Together they untied the strings and carefully removed the paper. Inside, on top of everything, were brightly colored jerseys. The children's eyes sparkled as Dr. Roseveare gave out the shirts. There were some knitted bandages for the leprosy patients. 30 pairs of eyes were focused on the box as a large container of raisins was brought out. That would make some good bread for the week end. Then the doctor reached in and felt. Could it really be? She pulled out a hot water bottle. She cried. She had not taken seriously Ruth's prayer. She had not truly believed that God would do this!

Ruth rushed up, yelling, "If God sent the bottle He must have sent the dolly too!" Rummaging around in the bottom of the box, she pulled out a small, beautifully dressed dolly. Ruth had never doubted. Looking up at the doctor she said, "Can I go with you to give the dolly to the little girl, so that she will know that Jesus really loves her?"

Because of mailing conditions, the doctor estimated that the parcel had been on the way to Zaire for several months. These things had been packed up by the doctor's former Sunday School class, whose teacher had heard the promptings of God to send a hot water bottle, even to the equator. One of the class members had even put in a dolly for an African child. This had all been done months before, in answer to the believing prayer of a 10 year old girl to "bring it this afternoon!"

God is not contained in time as are you and I. He is not hindered by the fact that one thing came before another. God sees all things as though they are happening now. In this case He saw and heard the little girls prayer before he guided the Sunday School teacher to send the box with the hot water bottle and the dolly. It was the same with the story of the wise men at the birth of Jesus. He saw the birth of Jesus before he lead the Wise Men to begin their journey, months before they needed to arrive with their own gifts for the baby in their story!

God knows what you will need even before you realize it yourself. That is another reason that we should not be afraid. As we face each day, let us get into the habit of trusting God to provide, just as He does for the birds of the air and the lilies of the field.

Let us pray: "Father, You know what we will face today. You know what we will need before we even know that we need it. Please give us this day, our daily bread, and whatever else that You think we will need. We will give You our thanks in Christ's name. Amen."

- This story can be found on the Internet at: http:///www.allaboutgod.net/profiles/blogs/god-does-answer-prayeramazing

CHAPTER 38: I AM WONDERFULLY MADE
Psalm 139: 14, Deuteronomy 33:27.

Let me tell you a funny story. A young man was practicing for a marathon and had run for miles out into the country. He was very thirsty and came upon a farm house with a farmer in the yard. He asked the man if he could have a drink of water, thinking that he could drink out of the outdoor faucet. The man said, "sure, Mister. I've got some of the best water in these parts!"

He took the boy around to the back of the house where there was an outdoor well with the bucket that was let down on a chain from a big crank. The farmer cranked the bucket down and then back up and the bucket was full of cool, clear water. The man took an old gourd dipper that was hanging by a string and dipped it full of the water and handed it to the young man. The young man took another look at the farmer, who had whiskers and a long mustache that drooped over his mouth. The mustache was dirty and covered with old tobacco juice. The young man quickly realized that he was about to put his lips where that dirty mustache had been. So he turned the gourd around awkwardly to the opposite edge and figured he was drinking safely. The old farmer clapped his hand to his leg and said, "By golly, you're the first fella I've ever seen that drinks from a gourd just like I do!"

Well, I know exactly how that young man felt. When I was about 9 years old, I went with my mother to visit her brother in the country. This was in the early 1940's and the uncle's house had the outdoor toilet and his water supply was a 5 foot square old fashioned open well at the edge of the back porch. The uncle took us out, at one point, for a drink at that well. As everyone else took their turn at the dipper, all sorts of things went through my head. My lips would go on that dipper after 8 other lips had just been there. Besides that, who knew how many frogs, tadpoles, bird droppings and other things resided in that water. I chose to remain thirsty all day long!

But you know, we live in a world that is full of frogs, tadpoles, and germs of every sort. There are new germs, like MRSA and new strains of flu and tuberculosis that come into our environment every year. We do not drink water after other people but do you realize that we do share the air we breathe with every other living thing around us? Now, honestly, I am not trying to be crude. I am just saying that the world that we live in is not, I started to say, "hospital clean", but actually a hospital has more germs than anywhere else.

So, just why am I sharing these unsavory facts? Mainly to point out the miracle of life itself. From the time that we are born, we are living in an environment of danger. Millions of infectious viruses and bacteria are not only around us but constantly invading our bodies. Yet God has made us so amazingly wonderful that our bodies are able to live for 70, 80, 90 years in a relatively healthy state! Isn't that amazing?

Just think of how many beats our heart makes in the course of 70 to 90 years! We have a wonderful network of bones, muscles, nerves, and blood vessels that last for all these years! God has built into our bodies a wonderful thing called an immune system. The moment any harmful alien body of any description enters the threshold of our body, through a cut or through breathing or in any other way, thousands of cells go to work to attack that alien and then clean up the results of the attack. This goes on constantly without us even knowing it.

Knowing that there would be times that our immune system would be overwhelmed or would break down, God has built into nature many potential medicines and remedies that will help our immune system to fight off the attacks from outside our bodies. Then God went further and gave mankind the ability to discover the medicines and remedies that He has built into nature. So the whole wonderful world of medicine and research was born. As new enemies of our health spring up, God raises up new research and new medicines are uncovered from nature.

So, yes, we live in a scary world of frogs and tadpoles and awful germs. A world of health and sickness and even death. But God has not left us defenseless. When our days are healthy He gives us strength and vitality and many challenges to meet. When our days taste of sickness He gives us the blessings of modern medicine plus His Presence to give us strength. When our day of homegoing is upon us, He comforts us and meets us with open arms at His gates. Indeed, as Ps. 139:14 says, "I will praise Thee, for I am...wonderfully made. In Deuteronomy we are reminded that "the eternal God is thy refuge, and underneath are the everlasting arms." Let us be grateful for health, for the power to recuperate in sickness, and for the loving and everlasting arms of God that will cradle us, hold us up, and when the time is right, take us home.

Prayer: "Thank you for making us with your amazing skill and wisdom and for keeping us and supporting us during the years that you give us on earth. In Christ's name, Amen."

CHAPTER 39: BEING GOD'S MESSENGER

Let me tell you a true story. A dozen years ago, a fellow that I trust told me this story that happened to him. When he told me this story it was still very fresh in his mind. It had only been a short time since it happened and you could tell that his life had been greatly effect by the event. I will let him tell it in his own words.

"When I first came to Augusta, I came from California by way of Atlanta. When I got on the plane in California, another man got on just behind me and sat down next to me. We introduced ourselves and the man said, 'that's it!' as though a light had gone on in his head. I wondered what he meant but did not say anything about it. We talked about many things and during the course of our conversation I mentioned some problems I was having about knowing which direction my life should go. I had been perplexed for some time. As I talked with this stranger, he seemed to have the answer to every problem that I had. It was amazing how wise and interested in me he seemed to be."

"We had talked almost constantly from California to Atlanta. It seemed that I had received clarification on every problem that had bothered me. When we got to Atlanta I asked about his address in Atlanta, as I really wanted to talk with him more in the future. It was then that he told me that he was not from Atlanta but from California. He had purchased a round trip ticket back to California. He said that God had asked him to take this particular flight and that there was a man that He wanted him to talk with. That is why he had inadvertently said, 'that's it' when we were introduced. He had sensed immediately that I was the right man. He said that this was not at all unusual and that God regularly directed him in such a way. When we got off in Atlanta, the man immediately searched for the proper plane for his return to California."

The young man told me that his whole life had been changed by God using a man whose faith was so strong that he would fly all the way across the country to talk with one man because God had asked him to do so.

After hearing this story I thought long and hard about how wonderful it would be to be used of God in such a way. Actually, the man on the plane was doing the bidding of God in exactly the way that it was done in New Testament times. Do you remember the story of Peter and his dream about unclean food?

In Acts 10, there is a story of a Centurion named Cornelius who had prayed to God for help. This was at a time , early in the Christian movement, when the followers of Christ still considered themselves primarily Jews. It was just assumed at that time that anyone who became a follower of Christ would have to become a Jew first. An angel of God told Cornelius to send some men to the house of Simon the tanner in Joppa and to call for a man called Peter. In the mean time Peter, who was visiting Simon, had a dream. In the dream God showed a sheet like vessel being let down from Heaven with many animals that Peter had been taught were unclean. God told Peter to eat some of these animals. Peter refused, saying that he could not eat such unclean animals. God told Peter not to call anything unclean that God had cleansed. Peter was confused, but it gradually became clear to him, after the men from Cornelius came to see him, that God was showing him that, from then on, Gentiles were to be received into the Christian fellowship WITHOUT first becoming Jews. These transactions and many others in the New Testament were very much like the transactions that took place with the man on the airplane.

So, wouldn't it be wonderful if we, as Christians in the twenty first century, were to practice doing just what the man on the plane was doing? I honestly believe that the only reason that this is not a common practice is that we simply do not EXPECT God to use us in this way. I believe that, if we were to ask God to give us such assignments that He would be delighted to do so!

I would like to suggest that, in your next prayer time with God, that you tell Him of your willingness to be used in this fashion. Ask Him to please start you out with small assignments (not a round trip across the country). Ask Him to help you to become more sensitive to His direction. Then, and this is very important, expect Him to give you a thought, like "it would be nice if someone would call Betty Smith, since she has missed church for two Sundays in a row". Then, when the thought "hits you", just check with God by saying something like, "Is this Your nudge

Lord? Do you want me to do the calling?" Then, if you get a positive feeling or perhaps you might even hear words in your head, like, "Yes, Please. That is what I would like for you to do." Then, by all means do it. You will be "off and running"and you will know that God is training you to be one of His messengers! Doesn't that sound worth doing? I think so!

"Dear Father, help us to see how exciting it would be to become your hands and feet and a spokesman for You while we are here on earth. In Christ's name, Amen."

CHAPTER 40: THE MAGIC EYE PICTURE

What would you say that this is a picture of? Are you stumped? (I am holding up a 5x6 piece of paper that looks like a flowery wall paper sample). It is a bunny rabbit! You think that I am pulling your leg, right? It looks more like a wall paper sample from about 1920, doesn't it? Well, it really is an example of what was known as a "Magic Eye" picture in the 1990's. Technically it is known as an autostereogram. Remember, if you hold it at a certain distance from your eyes and stare at it for a while, your eyes adjust and you suddenly see a hidden picture amidst the jumble of colored figures.

It is not something that you imagine. It is really there! In this one there IS a picture of a bunny rabbit! But, if you did not know the secret of how to see the bunny rabbit, you could have this as your wall paper for 20 years and never suspect that it was there. The trick, of course, is to do two things. 1. Believe that there is a hidden picture there that can be seen if you look for it, and, 2. Stare at the picture steadily for as long as it takes for the hidden picture to suddenly appear to you.

Well, this same "magic picture" effect can work exactly the same way with many things that we look at in our every day life. If we only look at them superficially – just on the surface – we might be missing some very important meaning hidden inside. This morning, for just a few minutes, I would like for us to look together at several such "magic picture"events.

The first Magic Picture is found in some of the stories in the Bible and in some of our typical Sunday School lessons in particular. Sometimes I look at some Old Testament stories and I find myself saying, "Do these stories really have anything to do with my life today – Samson killing 1000 Philistines with the jawbone of an ass, just because he feels insulted by them? But then I realize that a large percentage of the violence that surrounds our lives every day is due to the fact that mankind has, by and large, not learned how to control its anger. Just maybe, if we look beyond the surface of the Bible stories, we might see a hidden picture inside. In this case the hidden picture in the Samson story is that his violent reaction is as relevant as this mornings newspaper. We view his reaction throughout the Middle East and in our own city.

When we look at a story of young David, we see him fuming furiously. It is a story found in I Sam. 25. It is the time that David's little band of followers has been encamped beside the pasture of a rich man named Nabal. David's army has saved Nabal's sheep and shepherds on several occasions from wild animals which threatened their safety. Later, David's men run low on provisions and David sends a small group to ask Nabal for a neighborly lending of food to tide them over until they can replenish their supplies. Nabal's arrogant and ungrateful reply is for the men to tell David that he does not owe David anything so do not bother him again! David is so furious that he is about ready to separate Nabal from his life and devastate his property. But Nabal's wife, Abigail, hears of the situation and quickly sends many donkeys, loaded with provisions to David. She follows the supply train on her own donkey and pleads with David to spare her husband. She says something like, "Yes, he is greedy, arrogant, and unbelievably stupid! But he is the only husband that I have." This calms David down somewhat and then she adds a special blessing that melts David's heart and quenches David's fury. She says the words that I claim as one of my favorite verses. She says, "David, your soul is going to be bound up in the bundle of life with God forever!" David's fury, hatred, and violence is totally gone. Perhaps the hidden picture here is that it is possible to turn down the volume on mankind's hatred and violence when we learn to apply some of the wisdom seen in the actions of Abigail – compassion, diplomacy, humility, and reliance on God. It could be a beginning anyway! Maybe if we look steadily at any of the stories in the Bible we might be able to see the hidden picture in it!

Next, picture a worship service on a Sunday morning. I go into the service and look at the sermon topic and perhaps it just "doesn't turn me on" right away. I think, "I guess I am just not ready for church this morning!" But I reluctantly open a hymn book and begin singing the designated hymn and one phrase tugs at my heart and tears moisten my eyes. My whole mood is changed. I am suddenly ready for the sermon! God has, again, shown me the hidden picture - in this case just by way of one line of an old fashioned hymn.

I come home and it is a balmy day. After lunch we decide to sit on the front porch for a while and enjoy nature. Soon I begin to think about all of the things I should be doing, rather than just sitting and looking at nature. I am feeling just a little depressed about this and that – news in the Middle East, age lines, and the fact that my old body doesn't work quite as well as it used to. Then I see a lone bird, sitting on the telephone wire. I wonder about him. Does he have a a wife and family? Friends? Wouldn't it be awful to have nobody! I have been SO blessed with family and friends. Look at that hummingbird – trying so hard to get nectar from the feeder that I forgot to fill. But he keeps on trying. I don't even have to try. I have enough to eat and more. I am SO blessed!

These flowers under the tree are still so pretty – blue, white, and red. They'll be gone pretty soon with the cold weather just around the corner. That one flower has a broken stem – bending over, broken, but being itself as long as it can be. Does it sense that its days on earth are few? I guess it is content to be itself for as long as God lets it stay. Just like me! Thank you, God, for giving me life. Long life. Good life! Thank you for showing me another "bunny rabbit" in the magic picture of your beautiful world! It was just a lonesome bird on a wire, a frustrated hummingbird, a broken flower – a rather commonplace picture. But hidden within was a fresh look at how blessed I am!

THE END

DONALD C. HANCOCK

78057199R00075

Made in the USA
Columbia, SC
08 October 2017